CLEATS & EATS

SEATTLE / PUGET SOUND

a boater's restaurant guide to the

waters of Seattle & Puget Sound

By Lorena Landon

Printed and bound in United States of America.

Warnings/Disclaimers/Cautions

All locator maps, diagrams, and drawings, including but not limited to islands, bays, docks, landings, streets, and restaurants in this publication should NOT be used for navigation. Boaters are responsible for carrying all appropriate charts and maps for purposes of navigation along with timely tide tables and charts of currents and all necessary equipment and supplies. Boat owners and operators need to make their own determination as to the suitability of docks, buoys, and anchorage pertaining to their own vessel's length, weight, type, and other factors.

Information and comments in this publication regarding restaurants, facilities, and other businesses are for information purposes only and do NOT constitute an endorsement or recommendation of any kind. Information in this publication has been included as provided by restaurants, marinas, park departments, municipalities, fisheries, private organizations, visitor centers, and historical records. Although the author and publisher have made every effort to ensure the accuracy and completeness of information contained in this publication, we assume no responsibility for errors, inaccuracies, omissions, or any inconsistency herein. Any slights of people, places, or organizations are unintentional.

The author and publisher disclaim liability and responsibility to any person or entity with respect to any loss or damage caused or alleged to be caused, directly or indirectly, by the use and/or interpretation of any of the information contained in this publication. The author and publisher do NOT warrant the fitness, quality, security, or accessibility of the places, facilities, or businesses referenced herein. The reader should verify the information by contacting the restaurant, marine facility, docks, and other business establishments in this publication to make their own determination. This publication is about restaurants accessible by water and related information as we know or believe them to be and are subject to change without notice.

Published by
Woodland Cove Press
9805 NE 116th Street, PMB 7346
Kirkland, WA 98034
USA
425-894-6016
woodlandcovepress@att.net

ISBN-10: 0-9741380-5-3
ISBN-13: 978-0-9741380-5-3

Table of Contents

Preface _____ iii

Overview _____ iv

Navigating this Book _____ v

Reference Map _____ vi

Seattle Area Waters _____ 2

Central Sound _____ 108

North Sound _____ 174

Fuel Docks _____ 233

Index _____ 234

Preface

Recreational boating is a popular pastime in Puget Sound with a rich variety of cruising, including inlets, bays, and open bodies of water along with navigable lakes and rivers. Puget Sound is known to have the highest per capita boat usage in the country covering a variety of boating pursuits from sport fishing, water skiing, and scuba diving to power, sail, and human-powered craft. Seattle lies in the center of the Puget Sound region and sits between Elliott Bay and Lake Washington. Bainbridge Island and the Kitsap Peninsula are to the west. Whidbey Island, Possession Sound, and Admiralty Inlet are to the north and included in the Puget Sound region.

There are as many types of boaters as there are types of boats, but all have one thing in common and that is cruising with a purpose and destination in mind. "Cleats & Eats" helps the captain and crew get the most out of each destination by including unique restaurant venues along with fun local events and activities for a successful and enjoyable experience. The "Cleats & Eats" restaurant guidebook series is recognized in the boating community as a handy must-have on-board guide.

Acknowledgements

I would like to thank the following individuals and organizations for their continued support and interest in the "Cleats & Eats" boater's restaurant guidebooks: Robert Hale, author of the Waggoner Cruising Guide; Oscar Lind of Robert Hale & Co., Inc. nautical book distributor; Chuck Gould of Nor'westing Magazine; Armchair Sailor; Captain's Nautical; Peter Vassilopoulos of Docks & Destinations; Lora at Shilshole West Marine and many other friends who have provided their support.

A very special thank you is extended to my husband, Leonard Landon, for the excellent maps and dock diagrams produced for this book and to my son, Duane Landon, for maintaining the "Cleats & Eats" web site.

Cleats & Eats Overview

"Cleats & Eats" directs boaters to unique eateries and hidden gems located upland from community docks, exclusive restaurant docks, public wharves, and marinas, ranging from fine dining and romantic bistros to nautical restaurants and pubs in the Puget Sound region from Seattle northward to Port Townsend. You won't be left rudderless once you reach land thanks to "Cleats & Eats," the must-have restaurant and activities guide specifically written for boaters. "Cleats & Eats" includes breakfast, lunch, and dinner venues for planning your cruise as well as things to see and do once you reach your destination, including museums, unique shops, and local events. All the research and leg work has been done for the boater's convenience. "Cleats & Eats" boater's restaurant guide is well organized for easy reference.

The "Cleats" section for each landing includes:
- Detailed guest dock description and procedures
- Location of transient moorage showing where to tie-up
- Contact information for day-use and private guest moorage
- Length of stay information for free day-use docks
- Points of interest, including museums, local events, and local transportation
- Photos from the boater's perspective

The "Eats" section of each landing includes:
- Cafes, pubs, restaurants, and bistros accessible by boat
- Restaurant names, phone numbers, and type of cuisine
- Descriptions of individual restaurants include décor, cuisine, and hours of operation
- Street maps showing boater-centric restaurant locations
- Photos to give the reader a pre-view perspective of restaurant venues

Navigating this Book

Information in this guide is organized into three sections Seattle Waters, Central Puget Sound and North Sound (to include Possession Sound, Admiralty Inlet, and Saratoga Passage). Information within each section is conveniently organized into four elements, described below. Photos of landing destinations and restaurants are included throughout this guide.

Harbor / Bay : A general description of each bay or harbor begins each section of this guide and includes a description of surroundings, points of interest, and nearby restaurants.

ELLIOTT BAY
Bell Harbor Marina

Visiting Seattle by boat is a delight and is a great option for locals wishing to avoid the gridlock found on many surface streets and freeways in this metropolitan area. Bell Harbor Marina, located on Seattle's waterfront, offers hourly and overnight moorage with easy access to restaurants, parks, and museums. Look for the spire sculpture at the Harbor entrance. Hourly rates are $15 for 0-3 hours and $20 for 4-6 hours regardless of boat length, call ahead to check availability. Guests should report to the Office (kiosk) upon arrival to make payment and obtain a gate access code. If arriving after hours, use the self-registration payment box at the Office door and see the security guard for the access code. Office hours are 7am to 6pm during the summer months and 7am to 5:30pm in the off-season. Hourly spaces are marked and located along the main breakwater between "B&C" docks, between

Landing "Cleats": Details including short term and overnight stays for each dock, wharf, or marina are included in a tabular description (right) and related

Montague Harbour Wharf	250-539-2488
	Wharfinger
The Montague Harbour Public Wharf is located adjacent to the Marina and offers a 160 foot guest dock for short-term and overnight stays.	
Short-Term:	Short-term stays are available without charge up to 4 hours. Rates are posted for additional hours. Use self-payment station.
Overnight:	Overnight stays are charged as posted. Use the self-registration, payment box at the head of the dock. Anchorage in Montague Harbour is an option.

annotated diagram (left) of the harbor/bay locating each landing. Additionally, these diagrams locate area eateries.

Restaurant "Eats": Select individual restaurants are described including décor, cuisine, and hours of operation in a tabular

HARBOUR GRILL		
The Harbour Grill is managed by the Marina and is open during the summer months. The Store & Grill's large deck has great views overlooking the Marina and Montague Harbour, a great place to enjoy the morning with a cup of coffee and muffin. Lunch and dinner menu selections include salads, burgers, and appetizer platters like the smoked Salmon Pate, Garlic Prawns & Spring Greens, and the Hummus Platter with pita bread. Burgers are always a favorite like the Salmon Burger, Curried Chicken Burger, Garden Burger, and the Montague Burger.	Lunch, Dinner	9:30am-5pm Mon-Fri 9:30am-7:30pm Sat/Sun May - September Hours May Vary
	Price	Inexpensive - Moderate
	Outdoor Seating	Yes, Deck. Summer Months
	Contact	250-539-5711 (Marina)

STURDIES BAY RESTAURANTS			
Atrevida Galiano Inn	Beef, Duck, Lamb, Seafood	134 Madrona Dr	250-539-3388
Galiano Pizza	Pizzas	Island Delivery	250-539-5544
Garage Grocery	Groceries	14 Madrona Dr	250-539-5500
Grand Central Emporium	Breakfast, Burgers, Soups, Salads	2470 Sturdies Bay Road	250-539-9885
Martine's Thai	Noodles, Chicken, Seafood	14 Madrona Dr	250-539-4171
Max & Moritz	Burgers, Dogs, and Indonesian	Ferry Terminal (orders to go)	250-539-5888
Scoops Ice Cream	Ice Cream, Burgers	2470 Sturdies Bay Road	250-539-2488
Trincomali Bakery	Deli Sandwiches, Soups, Baked Goods	2540 Sturdies Bay Road	250-539-2004
Fly'n Bhun	All Restaurants	Delivery Service	250-539-8025

format (right). Towns of significant size contain a listing (left) of restaurants along with selected restaurants described individually.

Street diagrams: For towns of significant size, street diagrams are included in this section showing the location of restaurants to help the reader find their restaurant of choice.

Reference Map

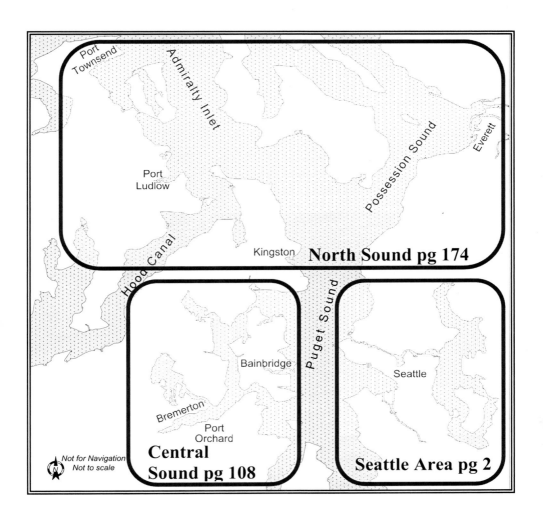

Port Townsend

Admiralty Inlet

Port Ludlow

Possession Sound

Everett

Hood Canal

Kingston

North Sound pg 174

Puget Sound

Bainbridge

Seattle

Bremerton

Port Orchard

Not for Navigation
Not to scale

Central Sound pg 108

Seattle Area pg 2

Lake Washington **3**
    Kenmore 3
    Kirkland Area 5
    BeachHouse Guest Dock 7
    City of Kirkland Docks...................................9
    Carillon Point..21
    Settlers Landing 25
    Leschi Landing 27
    Madison Park 31
    Renton...37

Portage Bay... **41**
    Agua Verde Guest Dock 41

Lake Union **45**
    Lake Union Area..45
    AGC Building Guest Dock 47
    Chandler's Cove Guest Dock 51
    H.C. Henry Pier 55
    Ivar's Guest Dock 59
    Rock Salt Guest Dock.....................................63
    South Lake Union Park...................................65
    Terry Pettus Park 69
    Yale Street Landing 73

Ship Canal.. **77**
    Fishermen's Terminal......................................77
    24th Avenue Landing......................................81

Elliott Bay **91**
    Bell Harbor Marina..91
    Elliott Bay Marina 95
    Seacrest Park..99

Shilshole Bay................................... **103**
    Shilshole Marina..103

Seattle Area Waters

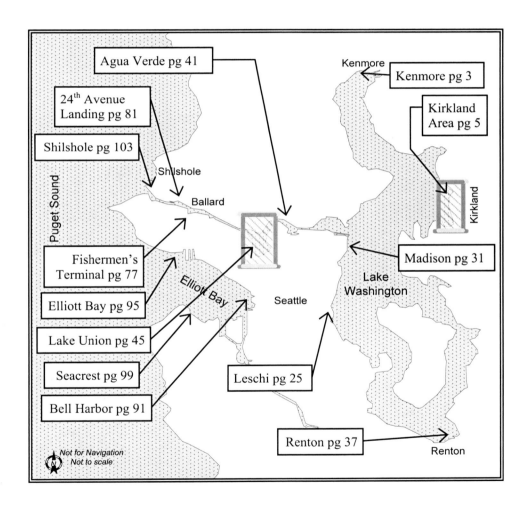

Agua Verde pg 41

24th Avenue Landing pg 81

Shilshole pg 103

Kenmore

Kenmore pg 3

Kirkland Area pg 5

Shilshole

Ballard

Puget Sound

Kirkland

Fishermen's Terminal pg 77

Elliott Bay pg 95

Lake Union pg 45

Seacrest pg 99

Bell Harbor pg 91

Elliott Bay

Seattle

Madison pg 31

Lake Washington

Leschi pg 25

Renton pg 37

Renton

Not for Navigation
Not to scale

LAKE WASHINGTON
Kenmore

This Kenmore City park with its public pier is located at the north end of Lake Washington, offering approximately 18 slips and ample side-tie for visiting boaters. The public dock sees very little use so space is most always available perhaps due to the shallow depths and high freeboard docks. When approaching this area of Lake Washington, stay clear of seaplanes arriving and departing from the Kenmore seaplane harbor facility. Fuel and marine supplies can be purchased at the adjacent Northlake Marina (425-482-9465).

Several eateries are just north of the public pier across State Route 522; use the crosswalk and light for safe crossing. To access the eateries from the Tracy Owen Logboom Park and Pier, walk north across NE 175th Street and the Burke-Gilman Trail, you will see a paved pathway leading up to the crosswalk at Route 522.

KENMORE RESTAURANTS			🍽
Acapulco Fresh Mexican Grill	Mexican Cuisine	6016 NE Bothell Way #D	425-482-0334
Everest Grocery & Deli	Groceries, Deli	6016 NE Bothell Way	425-402-0979
Jack in the Box	Burgers, Fish, Salad, Chicken	6100 NE Bothell Way	425-486-6856
Lakepointe Bar & Grill	Burgers, Salads, Sandwiches	18018 61st Ave NE	425-486-8021

ACAPULCO FRESH MEXICAN GRILL 🍽

The Acapulco Fresh Mexican Grill, located in a small strip mall on Route 522, is a great stop for a quick lunch on the north end of Lake Washington. This cute Grill with "Mexi" wall murals and décor serves burritos, tacos, tostadas, chimichangas, and salads along with side orders and combinations. Try the Baja Combo with choice of chicken, pork, or grilled vegetables with Rice Mexicanos, pinto or black beans, lettuce, and homemade guacamole and sour cream with three flour or corn tortillas;

Lunch/ Dinner	11am – 8:30pm Mon-Sat 11am – 8pm Sundays
Price	Moderate
Outdoor Seating	Yes, Sidewalk Tables Summer Months
Contact	425-482-0334 (take-out available)

or perhaps the Mexican Vinaigrette, a zesty house favorite with fresh romaine, cheese, and grilled vegetables with homemade guacamole and a honey-cilantro chili dressing.

LAKE WASHINGTON
Kenmore

The village of Kenmore was named by John McMaster after his previous home of Kenmore, Ontario in honor of Kenmore, Scotland. John McMaster was a prominent shingle mill operator in Snohomish and Kitsap counties and established the Kenmore McMaster Shingle Mill in 1901. The site of the Mill is at the present day "Associated Sand & Gravel Co." near Kenmore Air. While in the area, you might want to cruise up the Sammamish River, navigable by small/shallow draft, low-profile boats. Be sure to stay in the dredged channel as marked by buoys.

Tracy Owen Park Pier	425-398-8900	
	Kenmore Parks Department	

City of Kenmore park and public pier with 18 slips and ample side-tie (high fixed dock). Restrooms, no power or water on docks. Fuel nearby.

Short-Term: Day-use, no charge.
Overnight: No overnight stays.

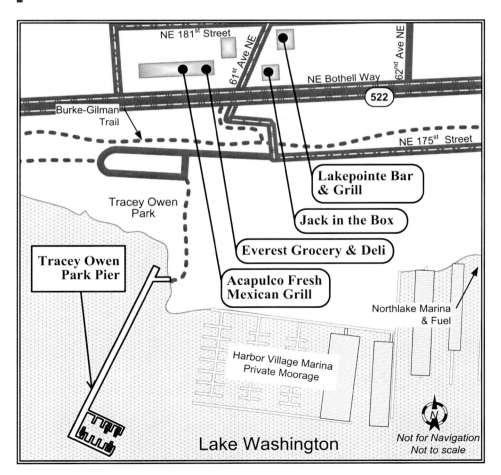

LAKE WASHINGTON
Kirkland

The city of Kirkland is without question one of the best destinations for hungry boaters. Located on the eastern shore of Lake Washington north of the 520 Bridge, Kirkland has commanding views of the Olympic Mountains and the Seattle skyline, offering numerous lakeside parks for sunbathing and picnic lunches. Kirkland is very boater friendly with several access points along its shoreline beginning with Carillon Point at the southern edge, providing hourly moorage for several restaurant venues. Proceeding northward a short distance you will find the BeachHouse Bar & Grill with its private dock used by patrons of the restaurant. Further northward is Settlers Landing, a street-end dock with short-term guest space on the north side of the dock and a pathway leading to the Pho Vietnamese Cafe. At the northern edge of Kirkland near the Argosy Cruise dock are two city of Kirkland dock facilities for hourly stays: the Kirkland Marina Park Dock(s) and the Second Avenue Dock. Both facilities are within steps of the heart of downtown Kirkland and its many cafes, coffee shops, boutiques, and art galleries. Overnight stays are permitted at the Marina Park Dock(s).

Kirkland takes its name from Peter Kirk, an enterprising businessman from England who headed to America in 1886. Peter Kirk came to the east shore of Lake Washington and built the Moss Bay Iron and Steel Works with the hopes of creating the "Pittsburgh of the West;" however, the mill was forced to close one year after it opened due to the financial panic of 1893. Around the same time, Kirkland became the site of the first wool mill in the State of Washington and produced wool products for prospectors of the Alaskan Gold Rush and later for the U.S. military during World War I. To learn more about the history of Kirkland, contact the Kirkland Heritage Society (425-827-3446) or visit them at 203 Market Street in Heritage Hall.

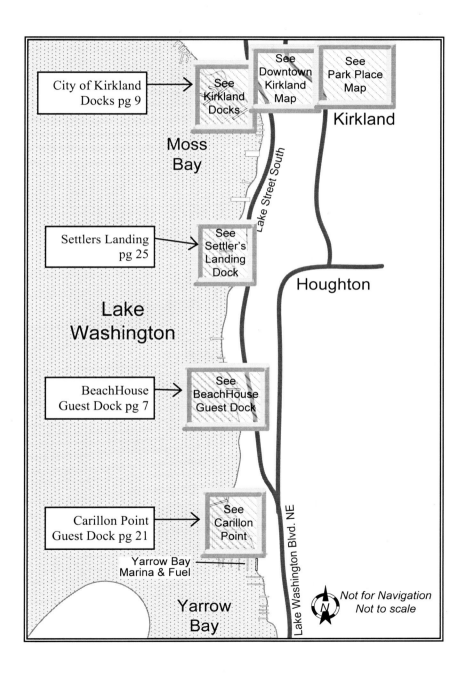

City of Kirkland
Docks pg 9 →

See Kirkland Docks

See Downtown Kirkland Map

See Park Place Map

Kirkland

Moss Bay

Lake Street South

Settlers Landing
pg 25 →

See Settler's Landing Dock

Houghton

Lake Washington

BeachHouse
Guest Dock pg 7 →

See BeachHouse Guest Dock

Carillon Point
Guest Dock pg 21 →

See Carillon Point

Yarrow Bay Marina & Fuel

Lake Washington Blvd. NE

Not for Navigation
Not to scale

N

Yarrow Bay

LAKE WASHINGTON
BeachHouse Guest Dock

The BeachHouse Bar & Grill, formerly known as Fiorente, is located between downtown Kirkland and Carillon Point. This venue offers beautiful views of Lake Washington, the Seattle skyline, and the Olympic Mountains in a casual setting. The restaurant's private 120 foot dock is available to boaters while dining at the BeachHouse. Spring lines are recommended as this landing is exposed to wind and waves.

BEACHHOUSE BAR & GRILL

The casual BeachHouse Bar & Grill offers dockside service so boaters can call ahead and have orders delivered directly to the boat dockside at the BeachHouse. The stunning views of the mountains and Seattle skyline can be enjoyed from window-side tables in the Grill or from the cozy booths overlooking the dining tables and water views. Menu selections include burgers, sandwiches, pizza, and specialty dishes like the Rib-Eye Steak and the Grilled Wild Salmon served with mashed red potatoes and seasoned veggies.

Lunch/ Dinner	11am – 10pm Sun-Thur 11am – Close Fri & Sat
Happy Hr.	3pm – 6pm and 9pm – Close Daily
Price	Moderate
Outdoor Seating	No
Contact	425-968-5587

For lunch, try the Grilled Turkey & Smoked Gouda Sandwich or the Buffalo Burger with Cajun spices, buffalo sauce, and bleu cheese. Appetizers are available in the bar along with wine, cocktails, and draft beers. The newly opened BeachHouse Bar & Grill has plans to add a breakfast menu on Saturdays and Sundays in the near future.

BeachHouse Guest Dock   425-968-5587
                                   beachHousekirkland.com

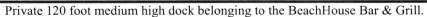

Private 120 foot medium high dock belonging to the BeachHouse Bar & Grill.
Short-Term: Short term stays while dining at the BeachHouse.
Overnight: No overnight stays.

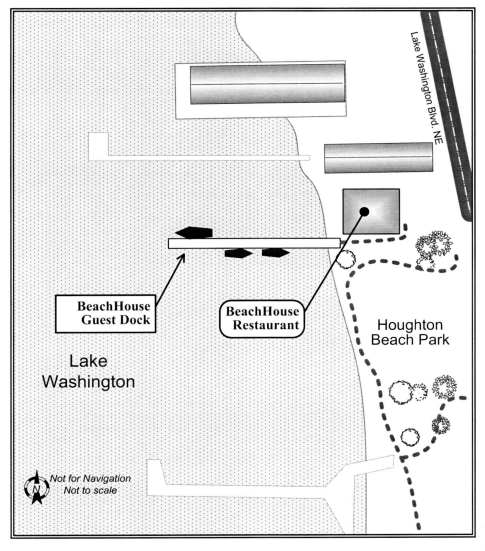

BeachHouse
Guest Dock

BeachHouse
Restaurant

Houghton
Beach Park

Lake
Washington

Lake Washington Blvd. NE

Not for Navigation
Not to scale

LAKE WASHINGTON
City of Kirkland Docks

The lakeside community of Kirkland offers boaters hourly stays at two main docks near the heart of downtown Kirkland: the Marina Park Dock and the adjacent Second Avenue Dock located between Anthony's Homeport and the Fish Café. Both facilities can accommodate most any size vessel and are on a first come, first serve basis. The first hour at both facilities is without charge for loading and unloading purposes after which payment should be made at the registration payment kiosk located at the head of the Marina Park Dock. The City of Kirkland has recently installed an additional pay station on the Second Avenue Dock. Transient space on the Second Avenue Dock is located on the south side of the dock and is for day use only. Daily moorage fees range from $7 to $15 or more based on length of vessel and day of week as posted. Overnight stays are permitted at the Marina Park Dock June through August with a maximum stay of 5 days. Boaters should keep clear of any commercial spaces marked in red and note yellow spaces, which are designated as loading zones.

Kirkland's upscale community offers numerous coffee shops, pubs, cafes, and fine dining venues. Most restaurants are within one to two blocks of the Kirkland docks. If you don't mind walking a bit further, you will find additional restaurants just east of the downtown core at Parkplace Center. To access these restaurants walk east on Park Lane through Peter Kirk Park to Parkplace. On Wednesday's, you can visit the Farmer's Market held in the 200 block of Park Lane from noon to 6pm, May through mid-October. During the summer of 2009-10 the Market will be held at the Marina Park due to construction in downtown Kirkland.

In addition to the numerous restaurants and wide variety of cuisine, Kirkland is popular for its many art galleries, spas, and unique shops. Be sure to stop at Sur La Table (425-827-1311) for all your kitchen and galley needs located at 90 Central Way and don't miss the SweetCakes Bakery at 128 Park Lane.

To tour the area, you can rent bicycles from the Kirkland Bicycle Shop (425-828-3800) at 208 Kirkland Avenue. For a truly unique adventure, try the seasonal parasailing offered by Pacific Parasail (253-272-3883) stationed at the Marina Park Dock.

Marina Park Dock	425-587-3340	
	www.ci.kirkland.wa.us	

City of Kirkland facility with 66 medium high slips and approximately 200 feet of side-tie, no rafting. Restrooms, no power or water at the docks. Launch ramp nearby used with a city permit access card.

Short-Term:	Hourly stays with fees as posted at the park kiosk, use self-registration payment box. Rates vary as posted.
Overnight:	Overnight stays June-Aug. with fees as posted with a maximum stay of 5 days. Use self-registration payment box, rates vary as posted.

Second Avenue Dock

425-587-3340
www.ci.kirkland.wa.us

City of Kirkland facility with approximately 400 feet of medium high side-tie, no rafting. Bathrooms nearby, no power or water at the dock.

Short-Term: Hourly stays with fees as posted at the park kiosk, use self-registration payment box. Rates vary as posted.

Overnight: No overnight stays.

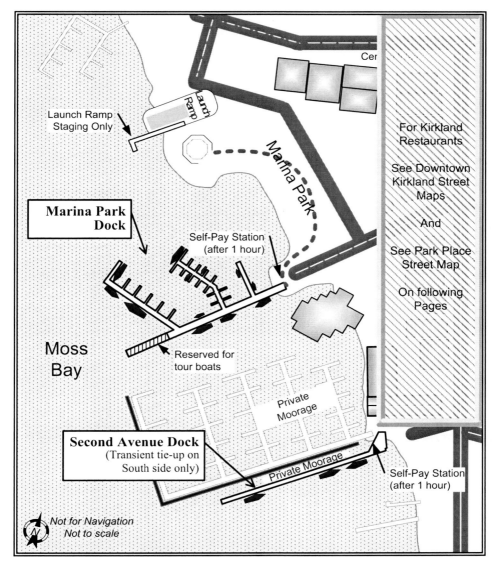

LAKE WASHINGTON
City of Kirkland Docks

KIRKLAND CASUAL DINING RESTAURANTS			
Cactus	Mexican Cuisine	121 Park Lane	425-893-9799
Café Happy	Asian Cuisine	102 Kirkland Av	425-822-9696
Coyote Creek Pizza	Pizza, Pasta, Salads	228 Central Way	425-822-2226
George's Place	Breakfast, Burgers, Greek, Pasta	108 Kirkland Avenue	425-827-6622
Hanuman Thai Café	Thai Cuisine	115 Central Way	425-605-2181
Hector's	Fish, Pasta, Steak	112 Lake Street	425-827-4811
I Luv Teriyaki	Japanese (To-Go)	104 Kirkland Av	425-739-8899
Jalisco Mexican	Mexican Cuisine	115 Park Lane	425-822-3355
Lai-Thai	Thai Cuisine	120B Park Lane	425-739-9747
Marina Park Grill	Brunch, Seafood	89 Kirkland Ave.	425-889-9000
Papa Johns	Pizza	211 Third Street	425-803-8000
Raga	Cuisine of India	212 Central Way	425-827-3300
Santorini Greek Grill	Greek Cuisine	106 Central Way	425-822-0555
Taco Del Mar	Mexican Cuisine	210 Main Street	425-827-0177
The Slip	Burgers, Fish Burger	80 Kirkland Ave.	425-739-0033
Thin Pan	Thai Cuisine	170 Lake Street	425-827-4000
Tiki Joe's Wet Bar	Burgers, Beer	106 Kirkland Av	425-827-8300
Tokyo Grill	Teriyaki	238 Park Lane	425-822-3473
VoVina	Martini Bar, Tasting	15 Lake St. #103	425-822-2221
Wilde Rover	Irish Pub Food	111 Central Way	425-822-8940
Wing Dome	Sandwiches, Salads	232 Central Way	425-822-9464
Zeek's Pizza	Pizzas, Salads	124 Park Lane	425-893-8646

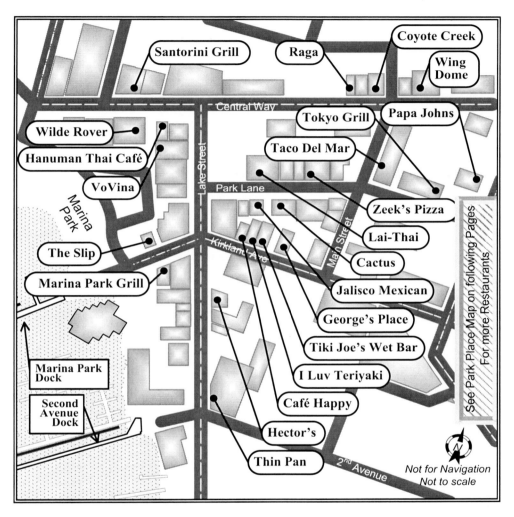

Santorini Grill

Raga

Coyote Creek

Wing Dome

Central Way

Wilde Rover

Hanuman Thai Café

VoVina

Tokyo Grill

Papa Johns

Taco Del Mar

Lake Street

Park Lane

Marina Park

Zeek's Pizza

Lai-Thai

The Slip

Kirkland Ave

Cactus

Main Street

Jalisco Mexican

Marina Park Grill

George's Place

Tiki Joe's Wet Bar

Marina Park Dock

I Luv Teriyaki

Café Happy

Second Avenue Dock

Hector's

Thin Pan

2nd Avenue

See Park Place Map on following Pages For more Restaurants

Not for Navigation
Not to scale

LAKE WASHINGTON
City of Kirkland Docks

KIRKLAND COFFEE & DESSERT			🍽
Ben & Jerry's	Ice Cream, Yogurt	176 Lake Street S.	425-576-1609
Caffe Ladro	Espresso, Pastries	104 Central Way	425-827-5838
Ce'fiore Yogurt	Italian Yogurt	111 Lake St. S.	425-889-5860
Coffee & Cone	Coffee, Ice Cream	1 Lake Shore Plaza	425-827-7098
Kahili Coffee	Espresso, Pastries	105 Lake St. S.	425-576-5600
Shnoo Yogurt	Yogurts	223 Kirkland Ave	No Phone
Starbucks	Espresso, Pastries	116 Lake Street	425-803-9086
SweetCakes	Bakery	128 Park Lane	425-821-6565
The French Bakery	Coffee, Baked Goods	219 Kirkland Ave	425-898-4510
The Grape Choice	Wine Shop	7 Lakeshore Plaza	425-827-7551
Tully's	Espresso, Pastries	164 Lake Street S.	425-803-0344

KIRKLAND FINE DINING RESTAURANTS			🍽
Anthony's Homeport	Seafood, Steak, Brunch	135 Lake St. S.	425-822-0225
Café Harlequin	Mediterranean	107 Lake Street	425-296-1616
Calabria Ristorante	Italian Cuisine	132 Lake Street	425-822-7350
Fish Café	Seafood, Lamb Steak	205 Lake St. S.	425-822-3553
Lynn's Bistro	French Cuisine	214 Central Way	425-889-2808
Market Street Café	European Cuisine	609 Market St.	425-827-4440
Ristorante Paradiso	Italian Cuisine	120A Park Lane	425-889-8601
Trellis	Beef, Duck, Steak, Seafood, Breakfast	220 Kirkland Ave Heathman Hotel	425-284-5800
21 Club	Steak, Seafood	21 Central Way	425-822-1515

LAKE WASHINGTON
City of Kirkland Docks

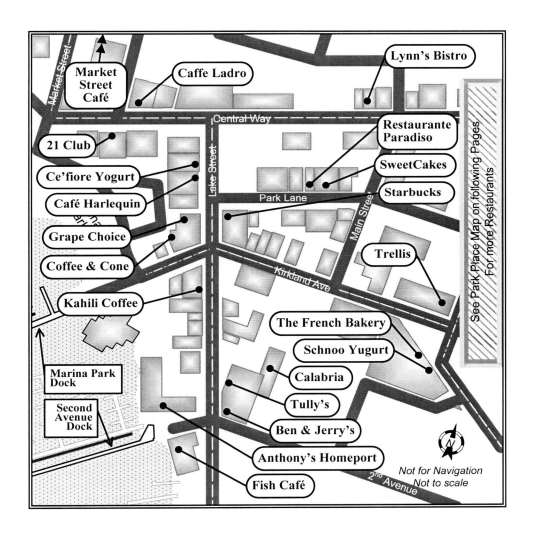

LAKE WASHINGTON
City of Kirkland Docks

KIRKLAND PARKPLACE RESTAURANTS 🍽			
Crab Cracker	Seafood	452 Central Way	425-827-8700
Emerald City Smoothie	Smoothies	512 Parkplace	452-739-9349
Hoffman's	Cakes, Pastries	226 Parkplace	425-828-0926
Lucia	Italian Cuisine	218 Parkplace	425-889-0200
Noah's Bagels	Bagels, Breads	320 Parkplace	425-827-7382
Purple Café	Seafood, Chicken, Pasta, Pizza	323 Parkplace	425-828-3772
Rikki Rikki	Sushi	442 Parkplace	425-828-0707
Saigon Jades	Vietnamese Cuisine	202 Parkplace	425-803-2991
St. James Espresso	Espresso, Desserts	355 Kirkland Av	425-968-2530
Starbucks	Espresso, Pastries	208 Parkplace	425-889-0293
TGI Fridays	Burgers, Pasta	505 Parkplace	425-828-3743
The Original Pancake House	Breakfast All Day	130 Parkplace	425-827-7575
Tim's Seafood	Fresh Fish Market	224 Parkplace	425-827-0195

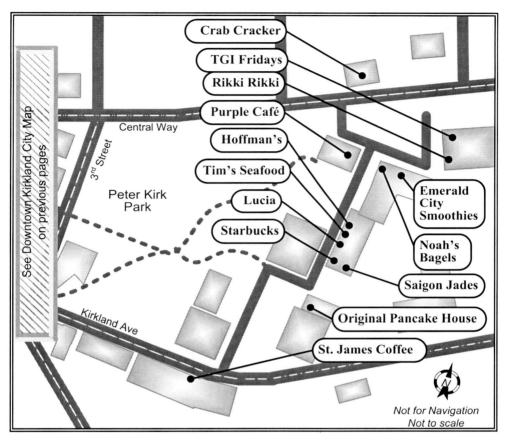

Crab Cracker

TGI Fridays

Rikki Rikki

Purple Café

Hoffman's

Tim's Seafood

Lucia

Starbucks

Central Way

3rd Street

Peter Kirk Park

See Downtown Kirkland City Map on previous pages

Kirkland Ave

Emerald City Smoothies

Noah's Bagels

Saigon Jades

Original Pancake House

St. James Coffee

Not for Navigation
Not to scale

LAKE WASHINGTON
City of Kirkland Docks

CAFÉ HARLEQUIN 🍽

Café Harlequin is one of Kirkland's newest restaurants, sporting dark wood furnishings, wood accents, classic paintings, and beautiful wall sconces. The Café specializes in Mediterranean dishes, including Moroccan, Italian, Greek, and Catalonian. The presentation is simple yet artful and chefs create all the breads, smoked goods, and confit. Starters include Duck Liver Pate, Crispy Calamari, and Steamers to name just a few of the excellent choices. For dinner try the Harlequin Smoked Chicken Fettuccini, or the Grilled Wild

Lunch	11am – 5pm Daily
Dinner	5pm – 10pm Daily
Lounge	4:30pm - Close
Price	Moderate - Expensive
Outdoor Seating	No
Contact	425-296-1616

Sea Bass served with braised potatoes, shallot, roasted tomato, olives, and capers. Lunch choices range from the lamb Gyro and the Prosciutto Sandwich to the Smoked Pork Tenderloin and the Crab Risotto. The Lounge offers food and beverage service throughout the day and breakfast selections are available on Saturdays and Sundays. Don't miss Harlequin's Jazz Nights held from 8pm to 10pm on the weekends.

FISH CAFÉ 🍽

The Fish Café is located on the third floor of the Chaffey Building at 205 Lake Street next to the Second Avenue Dock. The Café has dark warm woods, large picture windows, and a combination of tables and booths in a tiered fashion to take advantage of the beautiful views of the Seattle skyline, the Olympic Mountains, and the Kirkland Yacht Club Marina. Fresh fish is the entrée focus with additional offerings of steak, lamb, and chicken. Try the Seared Rare Ahi Tuna with black pepper fingerling potatoes, red onion jam, and toasted shallot oil, or try the Seared Alaskan Sea Scallops in a vegetable ragout and porcini broth.

Dinner	5pm – 9pm Daily Closing Hours Vary
Happy Hr.	4pm – 6pm 9pm – Closing
Price	Expensive
Outdoor Seating	No
Contact	425-822-3553

Delicious desserts and dessert wines provide the finishing touch. The separate bar is an ideal place to enjoy good appetizers or desserts during the special happy hour.

LAKE WASHINGTON
City of Kirkland Docks

RISTORANTE PARADISO

The Ristorante Paradiso in Kirkland, located on tree-lined Park Lane, is a romantic venue for lunch or dinner. The sidewalk patio and the interior Italian décor could serve as a scene from the God Father. Chef Fabrizio is originally from Triel on the island of Sardinia, Italy and creates special versions of traditional Italian recipes like the Cannelloni Gratinati, pasta crepes stuffed with ground veal, chicken, and mozzarella cheese in a tomato and besciamelle sauce; or try the Pork Tenderloin sautéed with mushrooms and sage in a Marsala wine sauce served with potatoes and vegetables.

Lunch	11am – 3pm Mon-Fri
Dinner	3pm – 10pm Mon-Sun
Price	Moderate
Outdoor Seating	Yes, Sidewalk Patio, Summer Months
Contact	425-889-8601

Stop by for linguine, pizza, or calzone for lunch; or try the Stracciatella Alla Romana, fresh spinach, parmesan cheese, and egg in a beef broth. Don't miss this Italian venue recognized by Zagat as one of the best.

PURPLE CAFÉ

The Purple Café and Wine Bar, located in Park Place Center, is a fun restaurant sporting concrete tables with iron furnishings and wall sconces on a brick interior. Lighting on the iron fence around the outdoor patio and the soft glow of interior lighting creates an intriguing ambiance. Wine racks in the restaurant display fine wines, which can be ordered by the glass or bottle. The Purple Café serves starters, salads, pizza & pasta, and sandwiches offered at lunch. Evening entrees include Braised Lamb and Peppercorn Crusted Ahi, or try the Chicken Marsala served with mashed potatoes and sautéed green beans.

Lunch/ Dinner	11am – 10pm Mon-Thur 11am – 11pm Fri & Sat
Price	Moderate - Expensive
Outdoor Seating	Yes, Patio, Summer Months
Contact	425-828-3772

Individual box lunches and cheese platters can be ordered for pick up (order by 5pm the previous business day), or stop by the Purple Café to enjoy appetizers, cheeses, and wine at the attractive wine bar.

WILDE ROVER IRISH PUB

The Wilde Rover is within steps of the waterfront and the Marina Park Docks, offering a large outdoor deck with lovely trees and umbrella tables for shade. This Irish Pub serves burgers, sandwiches, and traditional Irish fare like the Guiness Lamb Stew, the Shepherds Pie, and the Corned Beef & Cabbage, a slow roasted mustard glazed beef brisket, sliced and served with sautéed cabbage and champ potatoes. The salads are delicious and include the Wilde Salad with mixed greens, mandarin oranges, beets, red onions, and roasted pine nuts topped with citrus vinaigrette; or try the Apple & Goat Cheese Salad along with select draught beer or one of the Scotch blends, Bourbon's, or Irish drinks.

Lunch	11am – 4pm Mon-Fri
Dinner	5pm – 10pm Daily
Brunch	11am – 3pm Sat & Sun
Happy Hour	4pm-6pm and 10pm – 12am Daily
Price	Moderate
Outdoor Seating	Yes, Deck, Summer Months
Contact	425-822-8940

The Wilde Rover Pub is a popular venue for sports fans, who watch football, rugby, hockey, and soccer matches on the big screen television. Live music begins at 9pm throughout the week as scheduled. Come join the fun at the Wilde Rover Irish Pub.

LAKE WASHINGTON
Carillon Point

Carillon Point is Kirkland's upscale marine facility offering approximately 150 feet of transient moorage for a maximum 2 hour stay. Located on the eastern shore of Lake Washington at Kirkland's southern end, Carillon provides a great place to sit and relax, listen to the Carillon chimes, or stroll along the promenade. A Starbucks and five restaurants, ranging from casual to formal, await boaters and are within steps of the Carillon Point dock:

CARILLON POINT RESTAURANTS		
Beach Café	Seafood, Salads, Meats, Burgers	425-889-0303 #4
Bin Vivant	Breakfast, Seafood, Lamb, Sandwiches	425-803-5595 425-822-3700
BluWater Bistro	Seafood, Pizza, Burgers	425-822-4000
Poppinjay's Café	Sandwiches, Salads, Soups, Sweets	425-828-3048
Starbucks	Espresso, Pastries	425-827-2130
Yarrow Bay Grill	Seafood, Beef, Duck, Lamb	425-889-9052 #3

In addition to the great restaurants, Carillon is home to several high-tech companies along with a selection of retail shops and the Woodmark Spa (425-803-9000). The beautiful Woodmark Hotel (425-822-3700) offers first-class accommodations; and the neighboring, newly re-developed Yarrow Bay Marina (425-822-6066) has fuel, marine supplies, marine services, and boat rentals.

Carillon was once the site of a ship building yard and later the training facility for the Seattle Seahawks. Kirkland's ship building industry began with the construction of ferries. During the 1940's, more than 25 warships were built for the U.S. Navy at the Kirkland shipyard.

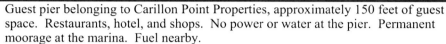

Carillon Point Guest Pier   425-822-1700
www.carillon-point.com

Guest pier belonging to Carillon Point Properties, approximately 150 feet of guest space. Restaurants, hotel, and shops. No power or water at the pier. Permanent moorage at the marina. Fuel nearby.

Short-Term: Short-term stays at no charge with a maximum stay of 2 hours.
Overnight: No overnight stays.

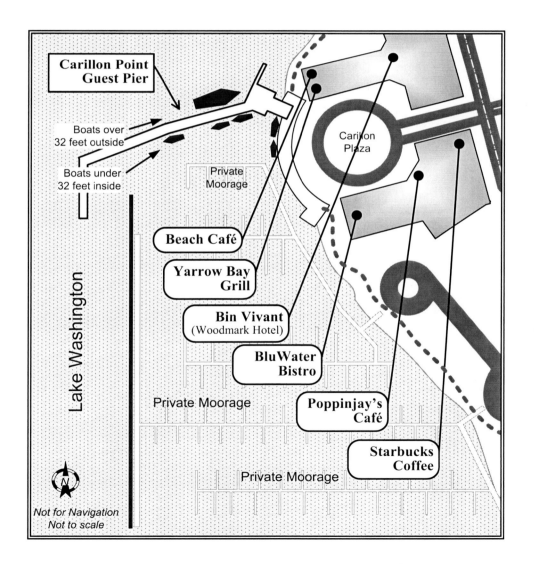

LAKE WASHINGTON
Carillon Point

BEACH CAFÉ   🍽

The Beach Café is a casual, chic lakeside venue offering seafood and meat dishes with a Mediterranean, Asian, and Southwestern flare, like the House Smoked Chicken Salad with apples, cranberries, and gorgonzola; or try the Baja Mahi Tacos with pickled jalapenos, salsa verde, and avocado. The outdoor wind-proof patio is set near the water's edge and is the perfect spot to view the marine activity on Lake Washington while enjoying a bowl of clam chowder, spicy crab cakes, and other seafood dishes like the Seven Spice Albacore with Asian greens and pickled ginger. Don't forget the Espresso Crème Brule or the Key Lime Cheesecake for dessert.

Lunch/ Dinner	11am – 10pm Mon-Sat 11am – 9pm Sundays Summers open till 11pm on weekends
Price	Moderate
Outdoor Seating	Yes, Patio, Summer Months
Contact	425-889-0303 #4

BIN VIVANT   🍽

Bin Vivant is located within the prestigious four-star Woodmark Hotel. The Bin Vivant, formerly known as Waters Bistro, is premised on pairing excellent wines with specialty dishes. Eighty climate controlled wines are available by the glass from the restaurant's large wine preservation system. Pinot Noir varieties are suggested for the Crabby Pig, a braised pork-belly served with Dungeness crab cake and pickled apples. Or try the Roasted Black Cod served with sushi rice, bok choy, and lemongrass Miso sauce with an Aromatic white wine.

Breakfast	6:30am – 11am Mon-Fri 7am – 2pm Sat & Sun
Lunch	11:30am – 2pm Mon-Fri
Dinner	5pm – 9pm Daily Open till 10pm Summers
Price	Moderate - Expensive
Outdoor Seating	Yes, Patio, Summer Months
Contact	425-803-5595

Comfort foods are offered at lunch like the Northwest Alfredo with smoked King Salmon, or try Steve's Blackened Sea Scallops with Russet Potato latke, seasonal vegetables, and lemon crème fraiche. Casual eats include burgers, sandwiches, and dinner salads. The patio is available during the summer months for outdoor dining, providing a majestic view of Lake Washington, the Olympics, and the Seattle skyline.

YARROW BAY GRILL   🍽

The Yarrow Bay Grill is located upstairs from The Beach Café and offers a cozy intimate venue with warm yellow and brown colors and great views from every table. Menus are printed daily and may include dishes like the Copper River King Salmon, Grilled Alaskan Halibut, Oregon Country Rib-eye, and the Anderson Ranch Lamb Rack with a hazelnut crust and pomegranate demi, served with chevre potato gratin. Smaller plates include the Crispy Duck Confit, Dungeness Crab Cakes, and the Kumamoto Oyster Duo. The Yarrow Bay Grill has a commanding view of Lake Washington, the Seattle skyline, and the Olympic Mountains and offers pleasant outdoor patio dining during the summer months with linen set tables, a romantic setting you won't want to miss.

Dinner	5:30pm – 9:30pm Mon-Sat Closed Sundays Closing extended 1/2 hour during summers
Price	Expensive
Outdoor Seating	Yes, Patio Summer Months
Contact	425-889-9052 #3

LAKE WASHINGTON
Settlers Landing

Settlers Landing is located about a half mile south of the City of Kirkland Docks and Argosy Cruise Dock. This street-end landing offers guest space on the north side of the dock; the south side is for private moorage only. Signage at Settlers Landing displays a 30-minute maximum stay; however, the City of Kirkland has indicated that longer stays while dining in the area are permitted as needed, day-long stays are discouraged. The Pho Yummy Vietnamese Café is located across the street from Settlers Landing and is a pleasant stop for a casual lunch or afternoon meal. The small street-end park with its lovely landscaping has an attractive pathway leading up to Lake Street.

PHO YUMMY VIETNAMESE 🍽️

Pho Yummy serves authentic Vietnamese noodle soups with a variety of meats, including pork, chicken, and beef. The BBQ Pork with peanuts, noodles, and egg rolls is especially "yummy." Vegetarians can opt for the appetizer rolls and the Vegetable-Tofu Noodle Soup. Eight tables are tucked in this small café with additional seating available on the patio during the summer months.	Lunch/ Dinner	10am – 9pm Daily
	Price	Moderate
	Outdoor Seating	Yes, Patio Summer Months
	Contact	425-739-9944

Settlers Landing	425-587-3380
	City of Kirkland

City of Kirkland dock with approx. 80 feet of guest space suitable for runabouts and cruisers.

Short-Term: Short term stays while dining at Pho Yummy.

Overnight: No overnight stays.

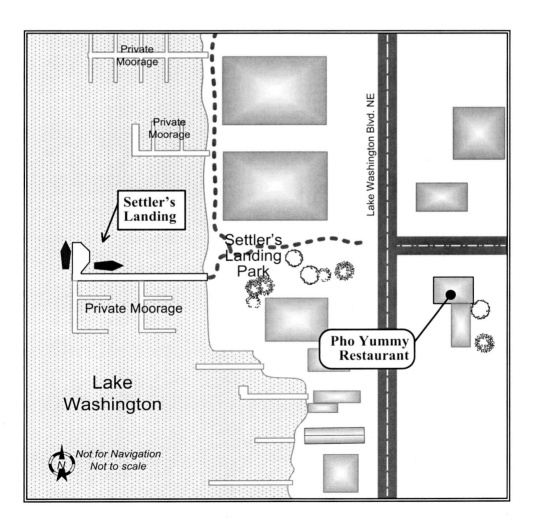

LAKE WASHINGTON
Leschi Landing

The tiny community of Leschi is a true gem located on the western shore of Lake Washington just north of the I90 Bridge. The L-shaped public float/dock is set behind a partial log boom and offers approximately 200 feet of guest space for a maximum stay of 2 hours at no charge. This medium-high float/dock is subject to heavy wave action so additional lines and fenders are recommended. Located just upland are several restaurants, a market, and a coffee shop:

LESCHI RESTAURANTS		🍽
BluWater Bistro	Seafood, Meat and Vegetable Dishes	206-328-2233
Daniel's Broiler	Steaks, Chicken, Lamb, Fish	206-329-4191
Leschi Food Mart	Groceries, Deli	206-322-0700
Pert's Deli	Sandwiches, Pasta Salads, Breakfast	206-325-0277
Ruby Asian	Thai, Japanese, Chinese	206-322-7288
Starbucks	Espresso, Pastries	206-720-4803

The shores of Leschi were once the campsite of Chief Leschi, who was appointed representative of the Nisqually, Puyallup, and Squaxin tribes for treaty purposes. According to some accounts, Chief Leschi refused to sign the 1854 Medicine Creek Treaty, which left a rocky piece of land to the Indians unsuitable for growing food and cut off access to fishing. The Indian tribes persuaded Leschi to act as war chief, and for more than a year skirmishes were fought between Indian warriors and volunteer militias of the U.S. Army, which became known as the Puget Sound War of 1855-56. Sadly, Chief Leschi was accused of murdering a soldier and was hung in 1858.

Today, the community of Leschi is a popular destination for beach goers and bicyclists, who stop to enjoy eats or purchase supplies at the two bicycle shops in the area.

Leschi Landing	206-684-4075	
	Seattle Parks Department	

City of Seattle public L-shape float/dock with approximately 200 feet of medium high dock. Restrooms in park, no power or water at docks.

Short-Term: Hourly stays at no charge with a limit of 2 hours.

Overnight: No overnight stays.

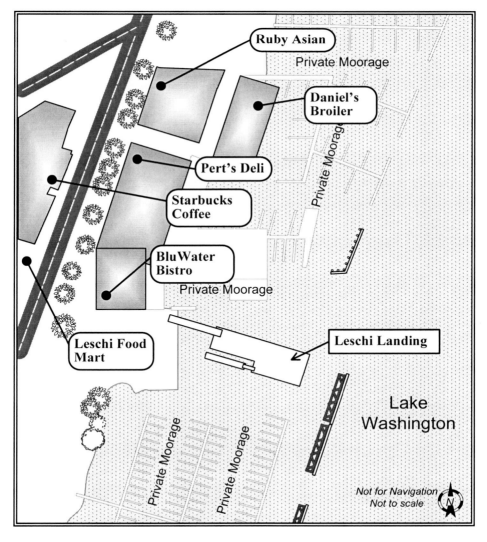

Ruby Asian

Private Moorage

Daniel's Broiler

Pert's Deli

Starbucks Coffee

Private Moorage

BluWater Bistro

Private Moorage

Leschi Landing

Leschi Food Mart

Lake Washington

Private Moorage

Private Moorage

Not for Navigation
Not to scale

LAKE WASHINGTON
Leschi Landing

BLUWATER BISTRO

This BluWater venue is a popular destination known for its open floor plan, fireplace, and cozy conversation areas. The seating arrangement for dining varies from intimate tables for two up to large round tables for group settings. The bar area has folding windows that open out to the summer patio from which diners can look through the restaurant out to Lake Washington. The good use of space has brought everyone together in an open friendly atmosphere. The same tasty and creative menu items are available here as offered at the Lake Union and Kirkland locations.

Lunch/ Dinner	11:30am – 1am Daily
Brunch	9am-4pm Sat & Sun
Price	Moderate
Outdoor Seating	Yes, Patio, Summer Months
Contact	206-328-2233

For dinner, try the Crab & Shrimp Stuffed Mahi oven roasted and drizzled with a macadamia nut burre blanc and a mango sweet chili coulis; or try the Prime Sirloin Meatloaf with tomato-barbeque glaze, served with country gravy and fresh mashed potatoes.

DANIEL'S BROILER

Daniel's Broiler at Leschi is housed in a renovated Boat House appointed with warm woods and beautiful chandeliers. The Leschi location, and all Daniel's Broilers, serves seasoned and seared USDA prime grade steaks, Filet Mignon, Rib-eye, Porterhouse, Top Sirloin, and New York steaks. Fresh seafood, chicken, lamb, and veal are also available. Daniel's serves award winning wines, and every Sunday night is "Prime Wine Night" with great wines at half price.

Dinner	5pm – 10pm Sun-Thur 5pm – 11pm Fri & Sat
Happy Hr.	4pm – 6:30pm Daily
Price	Moderate - Expensive
Outdoor Seating	Yes, Deck, Summer Months
Contact	206-329-4191

Daniel's at Leschi has the distinction of beautiful views of Mount Rainier, the Cascades, and the Bellevue skyline, which is especially stunning at sunset when the red glow reflects off the glass high-rises of Bellevue.

LAKE WASHINGTON
Madison Park

The charming community of Madison Park and the Madison public dock is located on the west bank of Lake Washington just south of the 520 Bridge, look for the tall imposing apartment buildings. The Madison dock is often missed by passing boaters assuming it to be private. Boaters visiting Madison may tie-up for 2 hours at the 60-foot, high-fixed dock without charge. The dock is exposed to wind and waves so spring lines are a must. Due to the height of the dock, ties here are challenging for runabouts and small cruisers but doable with the right technique. Boaters can use an anchor line off the bow (facing east) to hold the boat from drifting in and under the dock in addition to bow and stern ties, be sure your anchor is secure.

Madison is a delightful community and is worth the time it takes to properly secure your boat. The local shops and boutiques retain their 1920's-30's charm and a number of cafes offer European style outdoor seating. Don't miss the old-fashioned Madison Park Hardware shop (206-322-5331) on 42nd near the Thai Ginger and the kitchenware shop called "Cookin" (206-328-2665) next to the Cactus Café on East Madison.

After enjoying the delightful shops and eateries, visit the Pioneer Museum, which is open the second Sunday of each month from 1pm to 4pm located at 1642 43rd Ave. East, admission is free.

Madison Park was an amusement center in 1890 and was the location of Seattle's first baseball field. The park included carnival rides, an ornate boathouse, piers, and a wooden promenade. The "Mosquito Fleet" made regular stops for passengers at Madison Park. This land was set aside for public use by Judge John McGilvra, who cut a straight-line road in 1864 through the forest from downtown Seattle to Madison Park and is today the only direct route in Seattle between salt water and fresh water. John McGilvra also began a cable car route, which ran along Madison every two minutes during the summer months. If only we had such great public transportation today!

Madison Park Landing	206-684-4075	
	Seattle Parks Department	

City of Seattle 60 foot, high-fixed dock for public use at no charge with a limit of 2 hours. Restrooms in the park, no power or water at the dock.

Short-Term: Maximum stay of 2 hours without charge

Overnight: No overnight stays

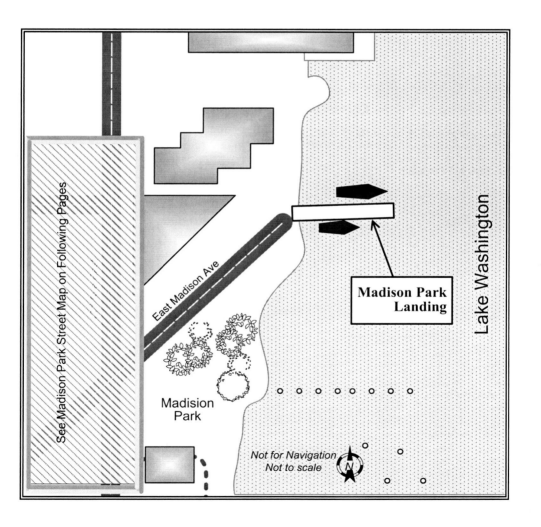

LAKE WASHINGTON
Madison Park

MADISON PARK COFFEE & DESSERTS			🍽
Madison Park Bakery	Cakes, Cookies, Pies, Pastries	4214 E. Madison	206-322-3238
Red Apple Market	Groceries	1801 41st Ave. E.	206-322-1330
Scoop du Jour	Ice Cream	4029 E. Madison	206-325-9562
Starbucks	Espresso, Pastries	4000 E. Madison	206-329-3736
Tully's	Espresso, Pastries	4036 E. Madison	206-329-6659

MADISON PARK FINE DINING			🍽
Impromptu	Steaks, Chicken, Fish	4235 E. Madison	206-860-1569
Madison Park Café	Beef, Duck, Chicken, Lamb, Seafood	1807 42nd Ave E.	206-324-2626
Sostanza Trattoria	Pastas, Seafood, Pork, Veal, Chicken	1927 43rd Ave E.	206-324-9701

MADISON PARK CASUAL RESTAURANTS			🍽
Attic Alehouse & Eatery	Burgers, Sandwiches, Salads, Pasta	4226 E. Madison	206-323-3131
Bing's	Burgers, Chicken, BBQ	4200 E. Madison	206-323-8623
Cactus	Mexican Cuisine	4220 E. Madison	206-324-4140
Mad Pizza	Pizzas, Salads	4021 E. Madison	206-329-7037
McGilvra's	Pizzas, Sandwiches, Pub Entrees	4234 E Madison	206-325-0834
Park Place Deli	Panini, Deli Salads, Quiche, Breakfast	4122 E. Madison	206-328-2492
Thai Ginger	Thai Cuisine	1841 42nd Ave E.	206-324-6467
The Red Onion	Pub Fare	4210 E. Madison	206-323-1611

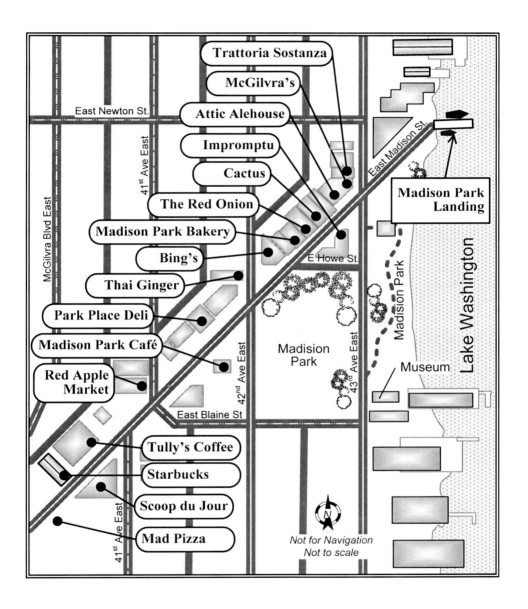

East Newton St.

Trattoria Sostanza

McGilvra's

Attic Alehouse

Impromptu

Cactus

The Red Onion

Madison Park Bakery

Bing's

Thai Ginger

Park Place Deli

Madison Park Café

Red Apple Market

Tully's Coffee

Starbucks

Scoop du Jour

Mad Pizza

McGilvra Blvd East

41st Ave East

East Madison St.

Madison Park Landing

E Howe St.

42nd Ave East

Madison Park

43rd Ave East

Madision Park

Museum

Lake Washington

East Blaine St.

41st Ave East

Not for Navigation
Not to scale

LAKE WASHINGTON
Madison Park

CACTUS

Cactus is a local's favorite and always draws a crowd of folks at all three locations; Madison, Kirkland, and Alki. The menu is devoted to "small plates" called antojitos, bocaditos, or tapas that are packed with flavor. This South American restaurant has brightly colored walls, furnishings, and décor that create a fun and festive atmosphere. Unique Cactus creations begin with the Grilled Jalapenos filled with herbed goat cheese wrapped in bacon and served with buttermilk crema; or start with a Tortilla Soup, or perhaps the Gambas al Diablo made with white Mexican prawns in a

Lunch	11:30am – 3pm Mon-Sun
Dinner	4pm – 10pm Sun-Thur 4pm – 11pm Fri & Sat
Price	Moderate
Outdoor Seating	Yes, Sidewalk, Summer Months
Contact	206-324-4140

spicy nectar served with cornbread. The tacos and entradas are equally unique like the Barbequed Skirt Steak & Poblano Chile Relleno made with crispy blue corn crusted chile, roasted mushrooms, sun-dried tomatoes, smoked Oaxaca, and cheeses served with sautéed seasonal greens and roasted pepper polenta in a sherry-tomatillo cream sauce with goat cheese crema. For a fun and unique culinary experience, be sure to visit Cactus.

IMPROMPTU CAFÉ

The Impromptu Wine Bar & Café is a true delight not to be missed. Chef Dan Ahern believes that living well means eating well. Each season, world-class wines are selected and paired with the monthly menu using fresh market ingredients. Wines on the menu are briefly described indicating the perfect match with cheeses, chicken, lamb, seafood, and spicy dishes for a complete sensory experience. Entrees may include Fresh Fish of the Day, Pasta of the Day, and other features like the

Dinner	5pm – 10pm Tue-Sat 4pm – 9pm Sunday (4pm Cocktail Service)
Price	Moderate - Expensive
Outdoor Seating	Yes, Patio, Summer Months
Contact	206-860-1569

Roasted Chicken with black rice, asparagus, and tamarind, or the Seared Lamb Chops with risotto-stuffed baby bokchoy, English peas, and mustard. Dan invites you to come relax at the classy bar, or at the white linen set tables, or outside on the lovely patio.

MADISON PARK CAFÉ

The Madison Park Café is located in a lovely 40's era home and is absolutely charming. The cobblestone courtyard is a popular venue during the summer months and earned recognition as the "Best Outdoor Brunch Dining" from Sunset Magazine. This intimate bistro serves fine wines and French style dinners like the natural grass fed Beef Tenderloin with roasted fingerling potatoes, green beans, and veal demi glace. Don't forget to start with the classic Onion Soup Gratinee or the Café Chicken Liver Pate.

Dinner	5pm – 9pm Tue-Thur 5pm – 10pm Fri & Sat
Brunch	8am – 2pm Sat & Sun
Price	Moderate - Expensive
Outdoor Seating	Yes, Patio Courtyard, Summer Months
Contact	206-324-2626

Desserts are a treat as well, including the Mascarpone Cheesecake, the Strawberry Rhubarb Tart, and the Chocolate Pave with raspberry coulis. You won't want to miss this adorable venue for brunch or dinner located at 1807 42nd Avenue.

LAKE WASHINGTON
Renton

The Gene Coulon Memorial Park, a Renton City park is located on the south end of Lake Washington. The harbor basin has 12 slips for boats up to 25 feet with additional space for larger boats along the inside east wall, a medium high fixed dock. Moorage is limited to 4 hours and there may be a wait for space during the busy summer months. An eight-lane boat launch is immediately south of the slips and seawall.

The exceptional design of Coulon Park provides covered outdoor picnic areas, gazebos, and boardwalks with additional tables and benches on floats. You can stretch your legs on the nature trails that run north and south along the Nature Island Sanctuary. Children love to run and play in the park, and after working up an appetite, enjoy a helping of Ivar's fish and chips or a Kidd Valley hamburger and milkshake. Parents should check out the "Annual Fishing Kids" program held at Coulon Park on the first weekend in June, open to children 5-12 years of age. Pre-registration is a must for this popular event where children receive instruction and get to keep their fishing rod and prize catch. Go to www.castforkids.org for more information or call the Renton Parks Dept. (425-430-6700).

Coulon Park was once an old ship storage facility. Gene Coulon, Director for 30 years of Renton Parks & Recreation, was instrumental in acquiring the first tract of land for this beautiful park. When departing Coulon Park heading north, be sure to take note of this unique location, where you can see the Bellevue city skyline and the Seattle city skyline from the same vantage point with Mercer Island nestled between the two cityscapes.

Coulon Park

425-430-6712
Renton Parks Department

City of Renton public facility with (12) 25 foot slips and approximately 100 feet of side-tie. Restrooms in the park, no power or water on docks. Launch ramp nearby.

Short-Term: Maximum stay of 4 hours; no charge.

Overnight: No overnight stays.

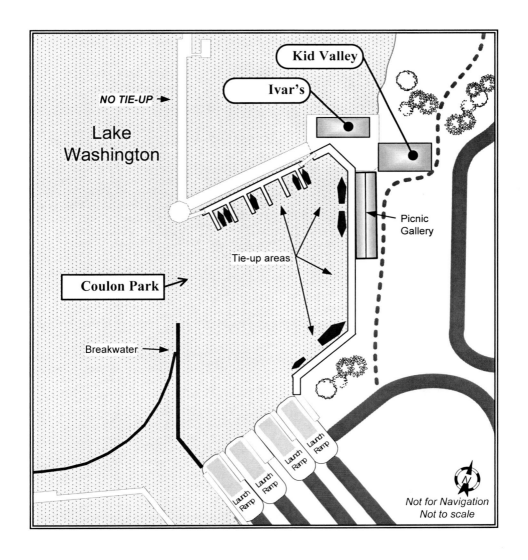

LAKE WASHINGTON
Renton

IVAR'S SEAFOOD BAR

Ivar's Seafood Bars share the same quality and history that the founder, Ivar Haglund began in 1938. Fish n' chips and the original clam chowder continue to be favorite Pacific Northwest treats enjoyed by many at this park with commanding views of Lake Washington and the Olympic Mountains.

Lunch/Dinner	10:30am – 8pm Daily Open till 9pm Summers
Price	Moderate
Outdoor Seating	Yes, Park Seating
Contact	425-226-2122

KIDD VALLEY

Kidd Valley's made-to-order burgers and hand-mixed shakes can be traced back to its founder John Morris, who had a fondness for tasty burgers and shakes. Morris sold his Kidd Valley restaurants to Ivar's in 1989. Kidd Valley burgers are made from fresh hamburger rather than frozen patties and the onion rings are made with fresh Walla Walla Onions in season.

Lunch/Dinner	10:30am – 8pm Daily Open till 9pm summers
Price	Inexpensive - Moderate
Outdoor Seating	Yes, Park Seating
Contact	425-277-3324

PORTAGE BAY
Agua Verde Guest Dock

The Agua Verde Café in Portage Bay has long been a best kept secret among local boaters. Portage Bay, located between Lake Washington and Lake Union, is home to the Seattle Yacht Club, the University of Washington, and many interesting house boats, which hug the southwest shoreline. The University of Washington owns the Boat Street Marina facility on the northeast bank of Portage Bay located in front of the Agua Verde Café. New docks were recently installed with the provision for two 25-foot slips designated for patrons of the Café. Signage is posted at the designated guest spaces; crew from the Agua Verde Paddle Club may be on hand to direct boaters to the appropriate spaces.

The new dock configuration at Boat Street Marina provides easy access and has good visibility so boaters can easily find this little gem. The Café is located in a green colored house overlooking the docks, while the Paddle Club is on the bottom floor at the water's edge. During the winter months, the kayak storage units are removed, providing four additional 25-foot guest slips. Vessels larger than 25 feet visiting the Agua Verde can anchor just west of the Café and come by dinghy to the Public Float located on the east side of the Boat Street Marina.

The narrow canal connecting Union Bay in Lake Washington to Portage Bay is known as the Montlake Cut and was first dug by hand in 1861 by Harvey Pike to provide a ditch for the passage of logs. In 1883, David Denny and Thomas Burke hired Chinese laborers to widen the canal in order to float logs from Union Bay to David Denny's Western Mill at the southern end of Lake Union. The canal as seen today was further modified in 1916 to accommodate boats and barges.

Today, the Montlake Cut is the site of the annual Windermere Cup crew races and Opening Day Boat Parade, which takes place on the first Saturday in May. Boats line the log boom in Union Bay and people line the banks of Montlake Cut for prime views of the event. Portage Bay is the terminus for the crew races and is where decorated boats congregate after the parade. Opening Day is sponsored by the Seattle Yacht Club; for more information and a schedule of events, go to www.seattleyachtclub.org/OpeningDay.

Agua Verde Guest Dock	206-545-8570

Boat Street Marina facility owned by the University of Washington with two 25-foot slips designated for patrons of the Agua Verde Café. Four additional 25-ft. slips available during the winter months. Anchorage nearby for larger vessels.

Short-Term: Short term stays without charge while dining at Agua Verde. Public Float for dinghies located east side of Boat Street Marina.

Overnight: No overnight stays.

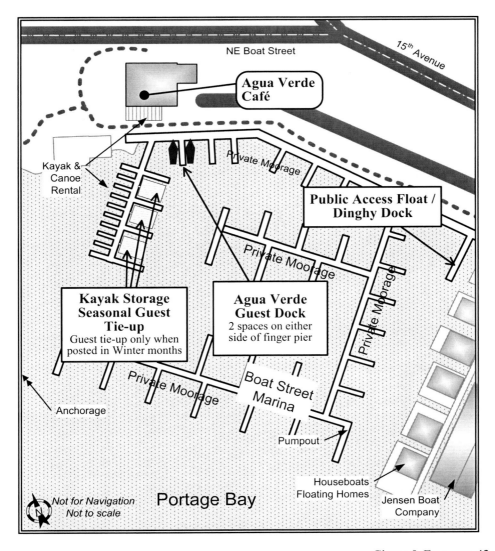

NE Boat Street

15th Avenue

Agua Verde Café

Kayak & Canoe Rental

Private Moorage

Public Access Float / Dinghy Dock

Private Moorage

Private Moorage

Kayak Storage Seasonal Guest Tie-up
Guest tie-up only when posted in Winter months

Agua Verde Guest Dock
2 spaces on either side of finger pier

Anchorage

Private Moorage

Boat Street Marina

Pumpout

Houseboats Floating Homes

Jensen Boat Company

Not for Navigation
Not to scale

Portage Bay

PORTAGE BAY
Agua Verde Guest Dock

AGUA VERDE CAFÉ	

The Agua Verde Café is a true delight housed in a home overlooking Portage Bay with its many houseboats. The interior of this lively café sports brightly colored walls, a decorative fireplace, and a heated, covered porch for year-round dining. The Café is filled with folks of all ages; and if you find a wait during the afternoon hours, you can order at the street-side window and enjoy your meal at the picnic tables in the adjacent park. The Agua Verde serves authentic Mexican foods with the Tacos de la Casa as their signature items along with house-made Margaritas and soft drinks.

Lunch	11am – 4pm Mon-Sat
Dinner	5pm – 9pm Mon-Sat
Happy Hr.	4pm – 6pm Mon-Thur
Take Out	7:30am – 2pm Mon-Fri
	Open Sundays, Summers
Price	Moderate
Outdoor Seating	Yes, Deck, Summers Adjacent Park Tables
Contact	206-545-8570

Try the Taco de Bagre with spicy catfish, lettuce, salsa Mexicana, and creamy avocado sauce, or perhaps the Boniato with sautéed yams, mild chiles & onions, cotija cheese, and avocado sauce. Dinner entrees include the Pollo en mole, chicken thighs in a sauce of dried chiles, Mexican chocolate, fruits, and spices served with cranberry slaw and creamy chile potatoes. Don't forget the Postres like the Mexican chocolate cake with prickly pear syrup.

LAKE UNION

Lake Union is nestled between Lake Washington and Elliott Bay with beautiful views of the Seattle skyline. Lake Union is considered the "sweet spot" of Seattle's boating community and is filled with marinas, parks, and numerous restaurants with public guest moorage for its many dining venues. You will find restaurants with guest moorage all around its shores if you know where to look. Some landings are hidden from view and transient space signage is sometimes lacking. The following pages include dock diagrams for each landing and its designated transient moorage space.

Lake Union is popular with tourists as well as boaters wanting to view its many houseboats, including the famous "Sleepless in Seattle" located on the northeast side of the Lake. The biotech industry continues to grow around Lake Union and includes the Fred Hutchinson Cancer Research Center and Zymogenetics, which is housed in the historic 1914 City Light's steam plant. The most popular event for boaters on Lake Union is the 4th of July celebration; a barge is positioned in Lake Union to launch fireworks and many spectators line the shores and vessels of every sort fill the Lake to capacity.

In early times, homes around south Lake Union became known as the Cascade neighborhood, which was settled by Russians, Swedes, Norwegians, and Greeks who worked in the area. The depletion of natural resources near Seattle and the Great Depression caused the neighborhood to decline in the 1930's. The approach of World War II slowed the decline and the U.S. Navy commandeered the site of David Denny's Western Mill for its Naval Reserve Center, which is now used for maritime events on south Lake Union. Kenmore Air (425-486-1257), also located in south Lake Union, offers flights to the San Juan and Gulf Islands as well as other destinations in British Columbia.

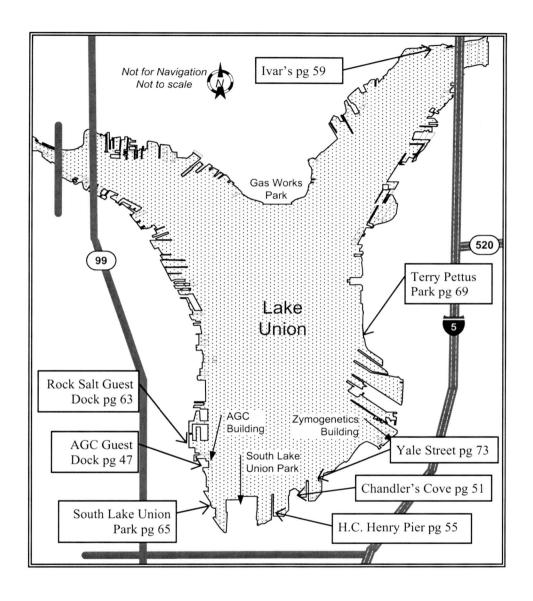

Not for Navigation
Not to scale

Ivar's pg 59

Gas Works
Park

99

520

5

Lake
Union

Terry Pettus
Park pg 69

Rock Salt Guest
Dock pg 63

AGC
Building

Zymogenetics
Building

AGC Guest
Dock pg 47

South Lake
Union Park

Yale Street pg 73

Chandler's Cove pg 51

South Lake Union
Park pg 65

H.C. Henry Pier pg 55

LAKE UNION
AGC Building Guest Dock

The AGC Building is one of the tallest buildings on the south end of Lake Union, and its unmistakable "AGC" in big gold letters on each side, make it an excellent landmark. The building offers tie-up space for guests at McCormick & Schmick's Harborside restaurant and Starbucks.

The tie-up area, located on the south side of the building, offers up to 85 feet of space and is well protected from wind and waves. Space is on a first come, first serve basis for patrons of McCormick & Schmick's and Starbucks. Both the restaurant and coffee shop are within steps of the tie-up area.

The Associated General Contractors of Washington (AGC of WA) dates back to 1922 and is the State's largest and oldest commercial industry trade association. The association has over 500 member firms, including general contractors and specialty contractors along with construction suppliers and services. AGC of WA includes the adjacent AGC Marina.

On the south side of the AGC Building and Marina is a ticket booth and launch for public cruises offered by Argosy Cruises (206-623-1445). This location includes a two-hour cruise of Lake Union and Lake Washington with narration featuring some of Seattle's famous places. Brunch, lunch, and dinner cruises are offered at the Elliott Bay location, which leaves from Pier 56. An Argosy station is also located on the eastside of Lake Washington at the Kirkland Marina Dock.

AGC Building Guest Dock   206-270-9052

Private AGC Building dock with guest space for patrons of restaurant tenants. No power or water at dock.

Short-Term: Short term stays while dining at McCormick & Schmick's or Starbucks.

Overnight: No overnights.

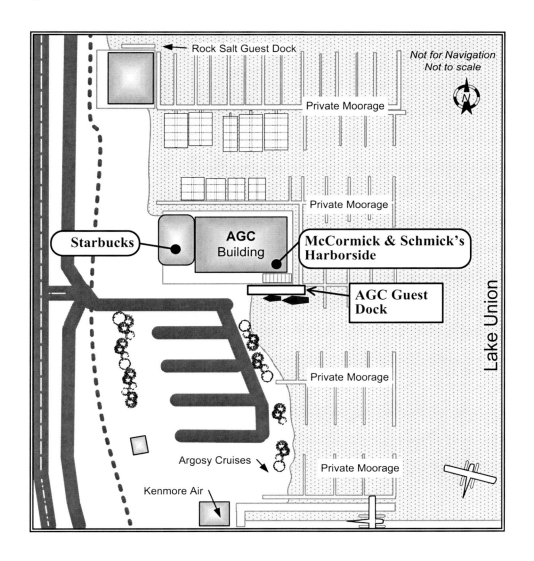

LAKE UNION
AGC Building Guest Dock

MCCORMICK & SCHMICK'S 🍽️

McCormick & Schmick's restaurants are well known on the West Coast and maintain a high standard. This nice restaurant with its warm woods and high ceilings offers a wide selection of fresh fish, including Oregon Petrale Sole, Trout, Salmon, Alaskan Halibut, and Hawaiian Albacore. Entrée choices also include steaks, chicken, and game hen. Specialties include the Thresher Shark blackened with rum butter sauce and tropical fruit salsa. The Columbia River Sturgeon seared and served over Granny Smith apples with sweet potatoes and bacon is another favorite. McCormick & Schmick's Harborside has one of the best views of Lake Union and the Seattle cityscape from its upper level restaurant.

Lunch	11:30am – 4pm Mon-Fri and Sat & Sun during May through August
Dinner	4pm – 10pm Sun-Thur 4pm – 11pm Fri & Sat
Brunch	10am – 3pm Sat & Sun
Price	Moderate - Expensive
Outdoor Seating	Yes, Deck(s) Summer Months
Contact	206-270-9052

The two lively bars, one on each level, offer high quality liquors and wines. A large selection of beers and other beverages are also available. McCormick & Schmick's is an excellent choice for brunch as well offering traditional and specialty breakfast selections.

STARBUCKS 🍽️

This Starbucks location is worth a special note regarding the great views of Lake Union and the city skyline from both inside the shop and from the summer patio and is a quick easy stop for the boater in need of a hot cup of coffee or a refreshing iced drink. Starbucks continues to expand with new shops and this AGC location is a favorite among boaters. The very first Starbucks opened in 1971 at Seattle's Pike Place Market, which has become a must see for fans of Starbucks.

Hours	5am – 8pm Mon-Fri 6am – 6pm Sat & Sun
Price	Moderate
Outdoor Seating	Yes, Patio, Summer Months
Contact	206-216-0306

LAKE UNION
Chandler's Cove Guest Dock

Chandler's Cove is located on the south end of Lake Union with a guest dock facility serving five restaurants:

CHANDLER'S COVE RESTAURANTS 🍽		
Chandler's Crabhouse	Seafood Focus	206-223-2722
Daniel's Broiler (see H.C. Henry Pier)	Steaks, Seafood, Chicken	206-621-8262
Duke's Chowder House	Seafood, Pasta, Burgers, Steak	206-382-9963
Hooters	Sandwiches, Salads, Chicken	206-625-0555
Joeys	Sandwiches, Burgers, Chicken	206-749-5639

Chandler's Cove 150 foot dock is on a first come, first serve basis for patrons of Chandler's Cove restaurants and merchants at no charge. Additional space suitable for runabouts is available on a 40' x 20' float at the north end of the dock. Boaters should note that this float is used by the Electric Boat Water Taxi (206-223-7476) from June to mid-September and is marked reserved during that time period.

The attractive plaza, shops, and restaurants at Chandler's Cove are a popular draw for boaters. It is best to arrive early on Friday or Saturday evenings during prime boating season.

The Puget Sound Maritime Historical Society (206-624-3028), located in the Plaza behind Duke's Chowder House, showcases photos and relics of maritime interest. Call ahead for the latest hours of operation.

Chandler's Cove Guest Dock	206-262-8820
	(Property Manager)

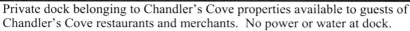

Private dock belonging to Chandler's Cove properties available to guests of Chandler's Cove restaurants and merchants. No power or water at dock.

Short-Term: Short term stays permitted while dining or shopping at Chandler's Cove restaurants and merchants at no charge.

Overnight: No overnight stays.

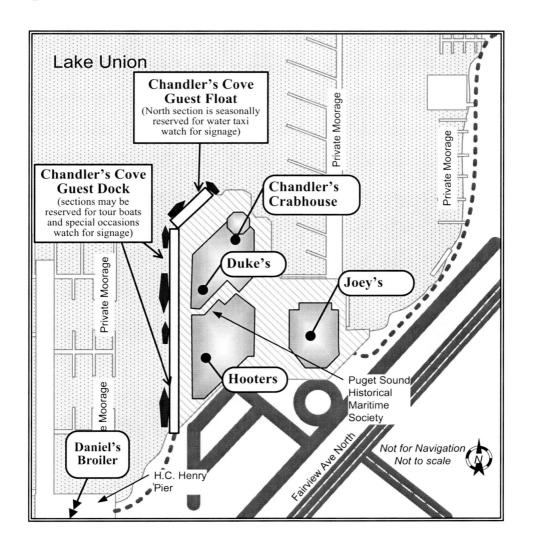

Lake Union

Chandler's Cove Guest Float
(North section is seasonally reserved for water taxi watch for signage)

Chandler's Cove Guest Dock
(sections may be reserved for tour boats and special occasions watch for signage)

Private Moorage

Private Moorage

Chandler's Crabhouse

Duke's

Joey's

Private Moorage

e Moorage

Hooters

Daniel's Broiler

H.C. Henry Pier

Puget Sound Historical Maritime Society

Fairview Ave North

Not for Navigation
Not to scale

N

LAKE UNION
Chandler's Cove Guest Dock

CHANDLER'S CRABHOUSE 🍽

Chandler's Crabhouse is one of the finest restaurants in Seattle offering great views of Lake Union from two lovely patios and from the floor to ceiling window-side seats. The seafood menu is superb and includes Dungeness Crab Legs, Ahi Tuna, Alaskan Halibut, and Copper River King Salmon served with fire-roasted vegetables and red pepper coulis; or try the Samish Bay or Fanny Bay fresh oysters or perhaps the Filet Mignon and Australian Lobster Tail served with garlic-mashed potatoes and grilled asparagus. Chandler's is a great choice any time of day.

Lunch	11:30am – 2:30pm Mon-Fri
Dinner	5pm – 9pm Sun-Thur 5pm – 10pm Fri & Sat
Brunch	10am – 3pm Sat & Sun
Price	Moderate - Expensive
Outdoor Seating	Yes, Patio, Summer Months
Contact	206-223-2722

DUKE'S CHOWDER HOUSE 🍽️

Duke's, a Seattle icon for more than 25 years, is a great place to enjoy a hot bowl of chowder on a cold, rainy Seattle day. Complete with a fireplace and picnic-style tables covered with blue and white tablecloths, you can choose from a wide selection of chowders, including clam, crayfish, crab & bourbon, salmon, shrimp, Cajun chicken, lobster, and Duke's northwest seafood chowder. If you find it difficult to choose just one, try the Chowder Sampler.

Lunch/ Dinner	11am – Midnight Daily Dinner menu begins at 3pm Bar stays open till 2am
Price	Moderate
Outdoor Seating	Yes, Deck, Summer Months
Contact	206-382-9963

Duke's also offers a nice selection of pastas, seafood dishes, burgers, steaks, and salads. Patrons enjoy the full service bar, which offers a good selection of beer, wine, and featured cocktails. During the summer months, you can relax on the open deck with nice views of Lake Union.

LAKE UNION
H.C. Henry Pier

The H.C. Henry Pier is the complex housing Daniel's Broiler located on the south end of Lake Union just east of the Naval Reserve building and the Center for Wooden Boats. Follow the channel between Daniel's Broiler and the Center for Wooden Boats to the shoreline. The tie-up guest space is on the south side of the last finger pier ('H' Dock) with 75 feet of space directly in front of Daniel's Broiler. Look for a small "Guest Moorage" sign on the end of the pier and the large "H.C. Henry" sign at the head of the pier. Guests may tie-up at no charge while dining at Daniel's for a maximum stay of 3 hours. If space here is not available, you may use the Chandler's Cove Dock while dining at Daniel's.

The pier's namesake, Horace Chapin Henry, came to Seattle in 1890 to work on the Northern Pacific Railroad's belt line around Lake Washington and later the Great Northern line from Stevens Pass to Everett. In 1909, H. C. Henry completed his contract to build a railroad line from Idaho over Snoqualmie Pass to Seattle. Around the same time, he began the Pacific Creosoting Company on Bainbridge Island in Eagle Harbor. H. C. appreciated the arts and constructed the Henry Art Gallery, which still houses his art collection along with other works.

H.C. Henry Pier   206-262-8820

Private H.C. Henry pier with 75 feet of guest space for patrons of Daniel's Broiler. No power or water at dock.

Short-Term: Maximum stay of 3 hours at no charge while dining at Daniel's.
Overnight: No overnight stays.

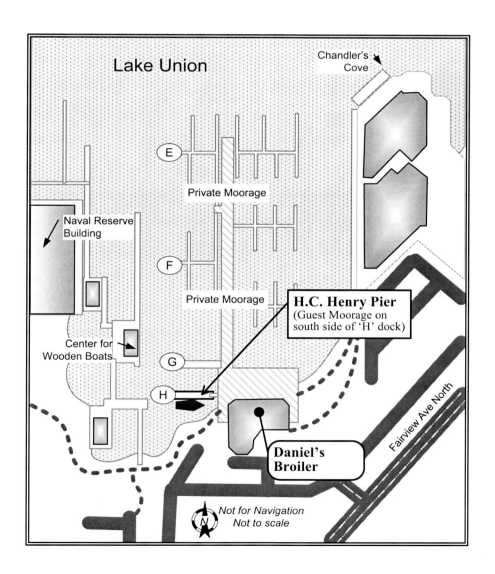

LAKE UNION
H.C. Henry Pier

DANIEL'S BROILER

For the steak lover, Daniel's prepares the perfect steak using only the top two percent prime cuts. Your steak is carefully trimmed and placed under a special broiler to lock in the flavor. Quality steaks include the Filet Mignon, Rib-eye, Porterhouse, Top Sirloin, and the New York, which are served with your choice of mashed garlic potatoes, baked potato, or rice and fresh vegetable. Other delicious choices include fresh seafood, chicken, and veal. Entertainment is offered in the piano bar during happy hour from 4pm to 6:30pm daily. This classy and beautifully appointed restaurant is every steak lover's favorite.

Lunch Dinner	11:30am – 2:30pm Mon-Fri 5pm – 10pm Sun-Thur 5pm – 11pm Fri & Sat
Price	Expensive
Outdoor Seating	Yes, Deck, Summer Months
Contact	206-621-8262

LAKE UNION
Ivar's Guest Dock

Ivar's Salmon House is the Seattle icon of dining by boat and has been receiving boaters for more than 30 years. Ivar's guest dock has a total of 160 feet and can accommodate most any size craft. Boats over 40 feet should tie-up at the east end of the dock in front of the concrete barge. The shore side of the floating dock is best suited for runabouts and smaller watercraft. The west end (inside) is reserved for the Electric Boat Water Taxi (206-223-7476) from June to mid-September. This is a popular destination, so on busy weekends and holidays you may need to wait for a space or raft up to another boat, which is customary at Ivar's.

Ivar's restaurants were begun by Ivar Haglund, a beloved Seattle character. In 1938 he established Seattle's first aquarium at Pier 54 along with a fish and chips stand and in 1946, opened the renowned "Acres of Clams" on the Seattle waterfront. Ivar loved singing and playing his folk songs based on his aquarium creatures Barney Barnacle, Hermit Crab, and Oscar & Olivia Octopus. In the 1950's, Ivar became a regular on KOMO TV's award winning children's program as first mate Salty on Captain Puget. Ivar Haglund passed away in 1985 but continues to be in the hearts and minds of many "Seattleites."

Ivar's Guest Dock   206-632-0767

Street-end dock offering guest space for boaters dining at Ivar's Salmon House and Fish Bar. No power or water at dock. A gate to the barge/dock is locked at or about 11pm.

Short-Term: Maximum stay of 3 hours while dining at Ivar's, no charge.

Overnight: No overnight stays.

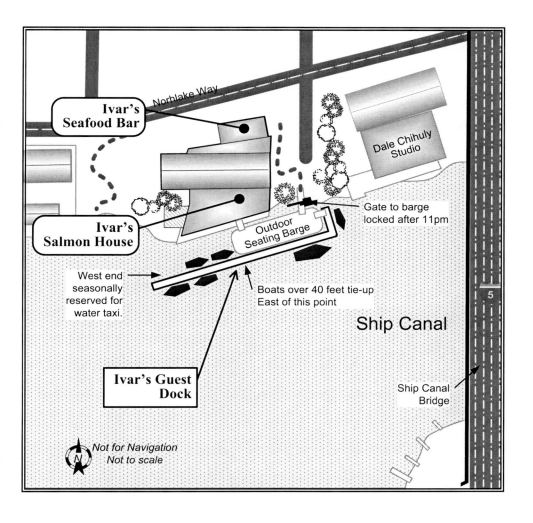

LAKE UNION
Ivar's Guest Dock

IVAR'S SALMON HOUSE

Ivar's Salmon House has one of the best views on Lake Union looking south toward the Seattle skyline. This is the place to savor Alder smoked salmon, a northwest tradition not to be missed. Other favorites include Alaskan Halibut, Jumbo Prawn linguini, and the Alaskan True Cod, which is stuffed with Dungeness Crab and Bay Shrimp, baked and topped with mariniere sauce. Ivar's on Lake Union is also a great venue for Sunday brunch or stop by the pub lounge for afternoon drinks and appetizers. A portion of the barge patio is reserved for patrons of the pub. The remaining portion of the barge is available for the Seafood Bar take-out.

Lunch	11am – 4pm Mon-Sat
Dinner	4pm – 9pm Mon-Thur 4pm – 10pm Fri & Sat 3:30pm – 9pm Sundays Pub open till 11pm
Brunch	9:30am – 2pm Sundays
Price	Moderate - Expensive
Outdoor Seating	Yes, Barge Patio, Summer Months
Contact	206-632-0767

Be sure to check out the historic photos of Seattle in the pub lounge and the artifacts and photographs of Native Americans displayed in the restaurant.

IVAR'S SEAFOOD BAR 🍽

Ivar's Seafood Bar is available at the take-out window located on the street side of the Salmon House building. The procedure for ordering at the window is to holler out your fish or chicken order, don't worry about the drinks, you take care of that when you pay. If you are unsure of the procedure, ask a local; they are more than happy to help. The Seafood Bar has year-round indoor seating next to the window, or you can dine at tables on the barge patio, or dine aboard your boat and enjoy the great view of Seattle.

Lunch/ Dinner	11am – 10pm Mon-Thur 11am – 11pm Fri & Sat
Price	Moderate
Outdoor Seating	Yes, Barge Patio, Rain or Shine
Contact	206-632-0767

LAKE UNION
Rock Salt Guest Dock

The Rock Salt Steak House is located on the south, west side of Lake Union and is an excellent option for hungry boaters looking to get away from the better known and sometimes crowded docks. Guests may tie-up on the 50 foot float located along the north side of the Rock Salt restaurant, which can accommodate runabouts and cruisers. Guest space is for patrons of the Rock Salt Steak House located a few hundred feet north of the AGC building. Look for the wide channel which lines up with the big red brick "Casey Family Building" on Queen Anne Hill. The restaurant is at the end of the channel.

ROCK SALT STEAK HOUSE	🍽️	
This comfortable restaurant has pleasant views of Lake Union from the lovely outdoor deck and window side seating. The Rock Salt restaurant is known for its prime rib, which is roasted very slowly covered in a blanket of coarse rock salt. Delicious char grilled steaks are also served, including the Chicago Rib-eye, the New York, and the Top Sirloin along with a nice selection of fresh seafood dishes and creative salads. Dinner entrees are served with fresh lemon spinach and garlic mashed potatoes. Lunch items include sandwiches, burgers, and pasta along with steak and seafood dishes.	Lunch	11am – 3pm Daily
	Dinner	4pm – 10pm Daily
	Price	Moderate - Expensive
	Outdoor Seating	Yes, Deck, Summer Months
	Contact	206-284-1047

Rock Salt Guest Dock   206-284-1047

Private dock for guests of the Rock Salt; a 50-foot float on the north side of the restaurant building. No power or water on float/dock.

Short-Term: Short-term stays at no charge while dining at the Rock Salt.

Overnight: No overnight stays.

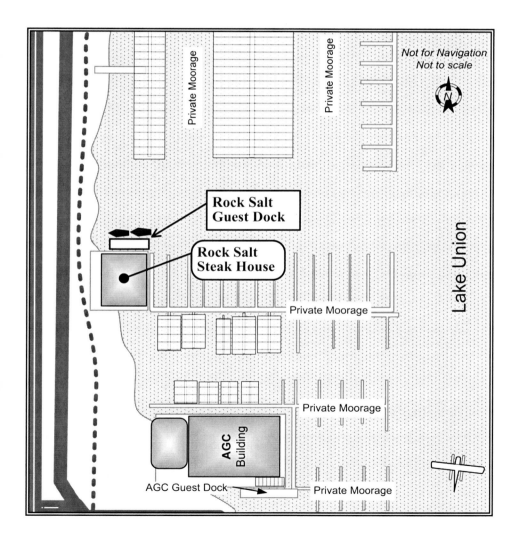

LAKE UNION
South Lake Union Park

At the time of this writing, the South Lake Union Park has entered the next phase of redevelopment, which is anticipated to be completed in the spring of 2010. The float located south of Kenmore Air will be for launch purposes only of non-motorized craft. Guest space for motorized craft is located along the L-shaped seawall on the west side of the Naval Reserve building. Guest space on this north/west seawall is by appointment; call the Center for Wooden Boats (206-382-2628) for space. The maximum stay of 4 hours is currently at $1.10 per foot and overnight stays are yet to be determined. The Naval Reserve building will be the future site for the Museum of History & Industry. For current information regarding the status and development at South Lake Union Park, call Seattle Parks at 206-233-3948 or the Center for Wooden Boats.

The Center for Wooden Boats (206-382-2628) hosts the Annual Wooden Boat Festival from June 30th through July 4th. You won't want to miss this collection of classic runabouts, speedboats, schooners, and working vessels, many of which are moored along the seawall directly in front of the Naval Reserve building. Workshops, displays, and smaller craft can be enjoyed at the Center for Wooden Boats museum docks on the east side of the Naval Reserve building next to Daniel's Broiler. Children love the hands-on activities at the museum, which is open year-round. Tugboat Story Time is held aboard the 100 year old Arthur Foss tug boat and features stories about boats, kids, and the sea. For more information regarding events and programs at the Center, go to www.cwb.org.

SOUTH LAKE UNION PARK RESTAURANTS		
Buca Di Beppo	Italian Cuisine	206-244-2288
Jillian's	Burgers, Pizza, Chicken, Fish	206-223-0300
Outback Steak House	Steaks, Pork, Lamb	206-262-0326
Tin Cup Espresso	Espresso, Pastries	206-464-7296

South Lake Union Seawall	206-382-2628 Center for Wooden Boats	

Seattle Parks Department facility under management of Center for Wooden Boats.
L-shaped seawall west of Naval Reserve building, Two 200 foot sections.
Signage and cleats located on the seawall, no power or water.

Short-Term: 4 hours at $1.10/ft. by appointment, call Center for Wooden Boats. Stays under 4 hours without charge at management's discretion.

Overnight: Overnight stays yet to be determined.

South Lake Union Park	206-233-3948	
	Seattle Parks Department	

City of Seattle public float 10' x 20' for small craft launching of kayaks and canoes.

Short-Term: Launch float

Overnight: No overnight stays.

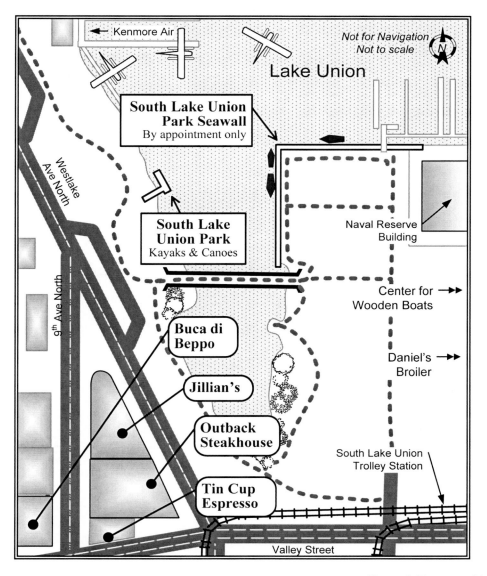

South Lake Union Park

BUCA DI BEPPO

Dinner	5pm – 10pm Mon-Thur 5pm – 11pm Fridays Noon – 11pm Saturdays Noon – 10pm Sundays
Price	Moderate
Outdoor Seating	No
Contact	206-244-2288

Buca di Beppo serves southern Italian fare on large platters meant to be shared. Exuberant portions of chicken cacciatore, veal parmigiana, garlic mashed potatoes, pasta dishes, and salads spill over the serving trays. The wood fired thin crust Neapolitan pizzas are especially good. For the lighter appetite, ask for the Buca per Due (for two), which is perfect for smaller parties. All of the wines at Beppo's are Italian and most are special ordered. The décor is as vibrant as the food with a fun whimsical combination of Rococo, Italian, Greek, and American icons.

You and your party will definitely have fun at Buca di Beppo ("Joe's basement") with its adventuresome series of dining rooms and its Italian community atmosphere. Buca di Beppo is located behind the Outback Steak House on the corner of 9th North and Roy.

OUTBACK STEAK HOUSE 🍽

The Outback Steak House has a rustic outback appeal with an Aussie theme décor consisting of boomerangs, kangaroos, and the like. Wood-plank, half-height walls define the dining spaces downstairs and the upstairs dining space has a separate bar and a patio area with great views of Lake Union. The Outback menu offers a wide variety of dishes from lamb, beef, and pork to chicken, fish, and pasta. Try the Outback Rack, a 14oz. rack of New Zealand lamb served with Cabernet sauce and choice of salad; or try the

Lunch	11:30am – 3:30pm Mon-Fri
Dinner	3pm – 10pm Mon-Sat 3pm – 9pm Sundays
Price	Moderate
Outdoor Seating	No
Contact	206-262-0326

Jackeroo Chops, two 8oz. center cut pork chops served with cinnamon apples and roasted garlic mashed potatoes. Don't miss the Walkabout Soup of the day, a unique presentation of an Australian favorite.

LAKE UNION
Terry Pettus Park

The Terry Pettus street end park is the perfect landing for runabouts, dinghies, and paddle craft. This 25 foot public float is located at the end of a channel between a row of houseboats and a row of large pilings just north of the old power plant on the southeast bank of Lake Union. Please respect the quiet privacy of the adjacent houseboats when approaching. Boaters may tie-up for 2 hours while visiting the park and restaurants in the area. The Azteca, Serafina, and Siam Thai are all within a short walk of the Terry Pettus Park float.

TERRY PETTUS PARK RESTAURANTS 🍽			
Azteca	Mexican Cuisine	1823 Eastlake Ave E.	206-324-4941
Serafina	Italian Cuisine	2043 Eastlake Ave E.	206-323-0807
Siam Thai	Thai Cuisine	1880 Fairview Ave E	206-323-8101

This street end park is named in honor of Terry Pettus, who lived from 1904 to 1984 and was an active political leader and newspaper reporter in the Seattle area. He became Washington State's first member of the American Newspaper Guild and he was a key organizer of the Seattle chapter. In his later years, Terry and his wife Berta lived in a houseboat on Lake Union and Terry Pettus helped form the Lake Union Houseboat Owners Association, now called the "Floating Homes Association." He was also instrumental in helping clean up Lake Union. At that time, houseboats had no sewer lines and the City of Seattle had 13 sewer outflows directly into Lake Union. Today, Terry Pettus Park reflects the namesake's desire to help create a sharing society and a clean environment.

Terry Pettus Park	206-684-4075 or 7249 Seattle Parks Department	

City of Seattle 25 foot float for small watercraft. No power or water at the float.

Short-Term: Maximum stay of 2 hours without charge.

Overnight: No overnight stays.

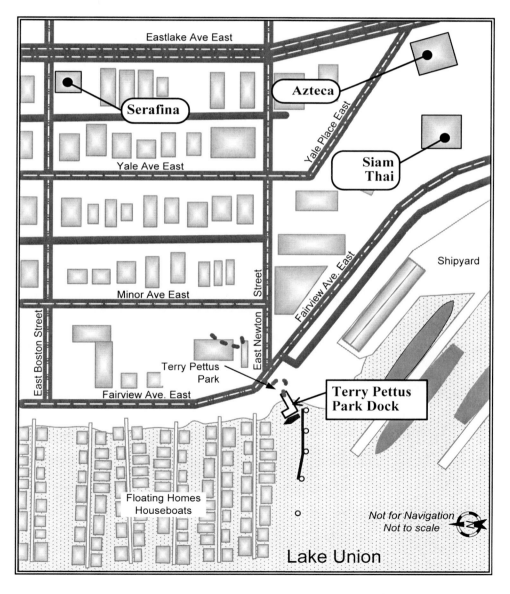

LAKE UNION
Terry Pettus Park

SERAFINA RESTAURANT

The Serafina Restaurant is about three blocks from Terry Pettus Park. Walk east on E. Newton Street until you reach Eastlake Ave. E. and turn left. Serafina's charming romantic ambiance makes this restaurant a perfect place for couples. Jazz groups and Latin ensembles entertain patrons on Friday, Saturday, and Sunday evenings, check the website for the latest schedule. Special wine tasting events with three-course meals are also noted on the website. Serafina serves country Italian fare reminiscent of Tuscany like the Plin, a handmade agnolotti filled with braised pork shoulder, savoy cabbage, and reggiano; or try the Polpettine di Vitello, house made veal meatballs simmered in a green olive-tomato sauce tossed with penne rigate and ricotta salata. Don't miss this top notch Italian venue.

Lunch	11:30am – 2:30pm Mon-Fri
Dinner	5pm – 10pm Sun-Thur 5pm – 11pm Fri & Sat
Brunch	10am – 2:30pm Sundays
Price	Moderate - Expensive
Outdoor Seating	Yes, Courtyard, Summer Months
Contact	206-323-0807 www.serafinaseattle.com

SIAM THAI CUISINE

The Siam Thai is about two blocks from Terry Pettus Park. Turn right from the head of the park and walk southeast on Fairview Ave. E. The restaurant is on the left-hand side on Fairview. Siam has long been known as one of the best Thai cuisine restaurants in Seattle offering three locations. The Lake Union location has a unique rustic appeal with train boxcar sides used as paneling along with an actual train boxcar for a portion of the restaurant. The authentic Thai dishes come with friendly service and generous portions. Favorite entrees include garlic prawns, pad Thai, and Siam special orange beef.

Lunch	11:30am – 3pm Mon-Fri
Dinner	3pm – 10pm Mon-Thur 5pm – 11pm Fri & Sat 5pm – 10pm Sundays
Price	Moderate
Outdoor Seating	Yes, Small Deck, Summer Months
Contact	206-323-8101

LAKE UNION
Yale Street Landing

The Yale Street Landing offers short-term stays for boaters visiting its two restaurants. Located at the southeast end of Lake Union with ample space, this dock is an excellent dining destination. Look for the BluWater Bistro sign on the building behind the kayak storage sheds. The Yale Street transient guest space is the entire H-shaped dock on the northwest side of the BluWater Bistro. Good backing skills will come in handy at this landing. There are 6 double slips that make a snug fit for two runabouts each, or one larger vessel. There are two shallow water spaces on the shore side of this dock. The deep-water end of the dock will accommodate larger vessels. Two dining venues are within steps of the dock:

YALE STREET LANDING RESTAURANTS 🍽		
BluWater Bistro	Seafood, Chicken, Steak, Sandwiches, Burgers	206-447-0769
I Love Sushi	Japanese Cuisine	206-625-9604

Yale Street Landing   206-292-1600

Private dock facility for guests of Yale Street Landing restaurants. Medium high fixed dock with six double slips and about 50 feet of side-tie. Backing skills are useful here. No power or water at docks.

Short-Term: Maximum 4 hour stay at no charge while dining at Yale Street.

Overnight: No overnight stays.

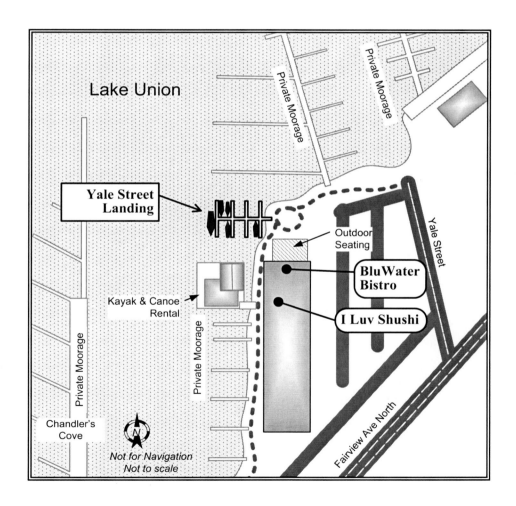

LAKE UNION
Yale Street Landing

BLUWATER BISTRO 🍽

The true bistro spirit can be found at the BluWater with its small cozy café and lively bar. The heated lakeside patio is very popular during the summer months and has great views of Lake Union and the Yale Street docks. The more formal upstairs venue can be reserved for Friday and Saturday nights. Sandwiches, burgers, and salads are popular choices for lunch, including the Portobello Mushroom Sandwich served on a Kaiser roll with provolone and roasted red peppers and basil mayo.

Lunch	11:30am – 4pm Daily
Dinner	4pm – 1am Daily
Price	Moderate
Outdoor Seating	Yes, Patio, Summer Months
Contact	206 447-0769

Dinner selections include steaks, chicken, and fish like the Citrus Salmon Fillet covered with lime, lemon, orange, and grapefruit then oven poached with white wine & butter, served with fried fingerling potatoes.

I LOVE SUSHI

Sushi lovers swear by I Love Sushi as offering the best sushi in town, the vinegary sweet rice combined with seafood and vegetables both raw and cooked. The white linen tablecloths provide a comfortable setting, while chefs in tall white hats prepare orders. Their Sashimi, strips of raw fish and shellfish are touted to be the freshest. For the timid, try the shrimp or the raw tuna with its mild, sweet taste, or the California roll of wrapped rice, avocado, and vegetables. Tempura, fish or vegetables cooked in a fluffy batter, is also available.

Lunch/	11:30am – 2pm Mon-Fri Noon – 2:30pm Saturday
Dinner	4pm – 10pm Sun-Thur 4pm – 10:30pm Fri & Sat
Price	Moderate
Outdoor Seating	Yes, Patio, Summer Months
Contact	206-625-9604 (take-out available)

For the more adventurous, try the Sea eel, salmon, yellowtail, whitefish, squid, and octopus. Presentations of these delicacies are always artful.

SHIP CANAL
Fishermen's Terminal

Fishermen's Terminal has been the home of the Pacific Northwest fishing fleet since 1913 with over 700 commercial fishing vessels. This historic location has a lovely bronze memorial in honor of those lost at sea as well as several plaques on local history. Guest moorage is available for up to 4 hours at no charge on the guest float located directly in front of Chinooks restaurant. To locate the guest moorage at Fishermen's Terminal, go south along the west side of the Ballard Bridge until you see the Fishermen's Terminal sign to the southwest, then turn west and follow the channel. Between docks '9' & '10', turn south. At the end of the channel you will see signs for guest moorage. As you pass, you can enjoy the wide variety of fishing vessels ranging from 30-foot gill-netters to 300 foot factory trawlers.

This interesting location has an excellent coffee shop and four eateries from which to choose or you can buy groceries at the Fishermen's Grocery Food Market.

FISHERMEN'S TERMINAL RESTAURANTS ⦿		
Bay Café	Breakfast	206-282-3435
Caffe Appassionato	Espresso, Pastries	No Phone
Chinooks	Breakfast, Seafood, Beef	206-283-4665
Fishermen's Grocery	Groceries	206-281-7818
Highliner Pub	Burgers, Fish, Sandwiches	206-283-2233
Little Chinooks	Fish and Chips	206-283-4665

If you would like to pick up some fresh fish to cook or freeze, don't miss the Wild Salmon Seafood Market located on the south side of Chinooks Restaurant. Visitors can also buy portioned fresh and frozen fish directly from local fishermen on Saturday's beginning at 10 or 10:30am. "Off-boat sales" occur along the west wall, a seawall that forms the western boundary of the boat basin at the Terminal.

Families enjoy the Fishermen's Fall Festival, which is held in September on the boardwalk of the Terminal with fishing theme activities for children and adults. Proceeds from the activities within the festival are donated to the Seattle Fishermen's Memorial Foundation (206-782-6577). On the first Sunday in May, the Foundation hosts a service to honor all those lost at sea and to add names on the plaques around the bronze Memorial.

Fishermen's Terminal	206-728-3395	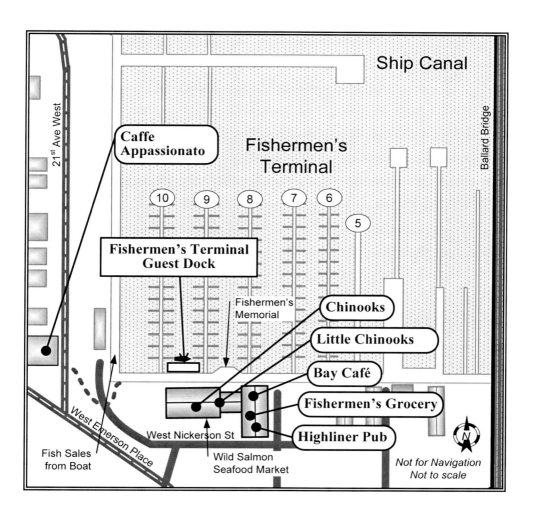
	Port of Seattle	

Port of Seattle guest dock for short term stays while visiting Fishermen's Terminal with approximately 125 to 135 feet of side-tie. No power or water at dock.

Short-Term: Maximum 4 hour stay at no charge.

Overnight: No overnight stays.

SHIP CANAL
Fishermen's Terminal

CHINOOKS

Chinook's at Salmon Bay is a casual, high-energy seafood restaurant located at Fishermen's Terminal. Salmon, halibut, and crab are the essence of Chinook's. Other fresh seafood entrees include trout, scampi, and oysters. Try the Alder Planked Salmon with sweet pepper sauce or the Fishermen's Cioppino. Although the specialty is fresh Northwest seafood, Chinook's extensive menu offers beef, chicken, and vegetarian fare. This great family restaurant sports a cannery motif and is popular with local fishermen and tourists alike. The large windows provide a great view of Salmon Bay and the Pacific Northwest fishing fleet.

Breakfast	7:30am – 11am Saturdays 7:30am – 1pm Sundays
Lunch	11am – 4pm Mon-Friday 11:30am – 4pm Saturdays
Dinner	4pm – 10pm Mon-Thursday 4pm – 11pm Fri & Sat 1:30pm – 10pm Sundays
Price	Moderate
Outdoor Seating	Yes, Patio, Summer Months
Contact	206-283-4665

Chinooks is home to the Husky Party Boat, which takes football game attendees from Fishermen's Terminal to the University of Washington Husky Stadium. For more information, call 206-283-Hook.

CAFFE APPASSIONATO

The Caffe Appassionato is a gem located near Fishermen's Terminal. Walk west from Chinooks through the west parking lot; you will find a worn path and a small set of stairs where folks cross 21st Avenue W. to the corner of West Emerson Place. You will find fresh, good tasting lattes and espressos here as Caffe Appassionato roasts their own coffee beans in-house, where you can watch the roasting process. Their process has been perfected to produce full-bodied, aromatic coffee that is less acidic and gentle on the stomach.

Hours	6am – 6pm Mon-Fri 7am – 4pm Sat & Sun
Price	Moderate
Outdoor Seating	Yes, Patio, Summer Months
Contact	No Phone

The attractive building has a lovely arbor entrance for summer outdoor seating. The building has beautiful mahogany wood pillars and sectional arched ceiling work on the interior and once served as a boat engine house in earlier times.

SHIP CANAL
24th Avenue Landing

Ballard's 24th Avenue Landing is a community constructed and maintained public dock offering boaters access to the Ballard community. Repairs to the dock are on-going and take place in May or June with volunteer help. Vessels 40 feet and under are welcome to tie-up and visit the area restaurants, shops, and markets located within easy walking distance.

Although the posted sign at the dock indicates a 2 hour stay, it is intended to discourage overnight stays per the Ballard Community Management Office. Stays during the day are at no charge. For overnight stays, contact nearby Shilshole Marina (206-728-3006). Plans are underway for a new park just upland from the Ballard dock along with a new 185-room "Point of Shilshole" hotel.

Ballard has come a long way since its early days as a Scandinavian community named after Captain William Ballard. Ballard has come in to its own with chic lounges, cafes, and fine dining restaurants along with new town homes, shops, and boutiques. Many of the brick and wood buildings in "Old Ballard" along Ballard Avenue date back to the late 1800's, and are being refurbished.

A Farmer's Market is held every Sunday from 10am to 3pm in early May through November located along Ballard Avenue. Other events include the Norwegian Constitution Day Parade in May and the Annual Ballard Seafood Fest in late July.

If you are interested in history, don't miss the Nordic Heritage Museum (206-789-5707) at 3014 NW 67th Street accessible by Metro bus #17 at NW Market Street in Ballard. The bus stop/drop for the Museum is at 32nd Ave. & NW 65th Street, walk two blocks north on 32nd and turn right on 67th to reach the Museum, which is open 10am to 4pm, Tue-Sat and noon to 4pm on Sundays.

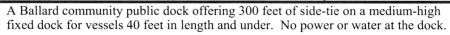

24th Avenue Landing	206-684-4060
	Ballard Community Dock

A Ballard community public dock offering 300 feet of side-tie on a medium-high fixed dock for vessels 40 feet in length and under. No power or water at the dock.

Short-Term: Short-term stays permitted during the day without charge while visiting the community of Ballard.

Overnight: No overnight stays.

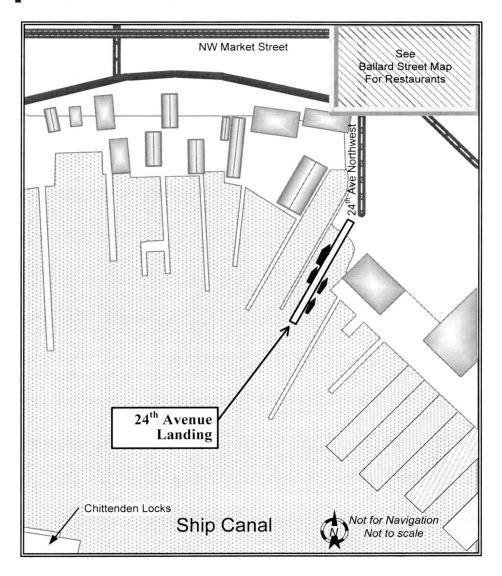

SHIP CANAL
24th Avenue Landing

24TH AVENUE CASUAL DINING			🍽
Anne's Teriyaki	Japanese Cuisine	2246 NW Market	206-789-5838
Azteca Mexican	Mexican Cuisine	2319 NW Market	206-782-7079
Bal Mar Lounge	"Lite Fare"	5449 Ballard Ave	206-297-0500
Great Harvest	Soup, Sandwiches	2218 NW Market	206-706-3434
Hamburger Harry's	Burgers, Beer, Sandwiches	2409 NW Market	206-297-8000
Hi-Life	Pizza, Sandwiches	5425 Russell Ave	206-784-7272
LaIsla	Puerto Rican Cuisine	2320 NW Market	206-789-0516
Madame K's	Pizza, Pasta	5327 Ballard Ave	206-783-9710
Matador	Burgers, Sandwiches	2221 NW Market	206-297-2855
Moshi Moshi	Sushi, Japanese	5324 Ballard NW	206-971-7424
Oayaca	Mexican Cuisine	5431 Ballard Ave	206-782-8722
Ocho	Spanish Tapas	2325 NW Market	206-784-0699
Old Town Ale	Pastas, Sandwiches	5233 Ballard Ave	206-782-8323
O'Shun Sushi	Japanese Cuisine	5809 24th Ave NW	New
Other Coast Café	Sandwiches	5315 Ballard Ave	206-789-0936
People's Pub	Pub Fare	5429 Ballard Ave	206-783-6521
Pho Than	Thai Cuisine	2021 NW Market	206-782-5715
Root Table	South Pacific	2213 NW Market	206-420-3214
Sam's Sushi	Japanese Cuisine	5506 22nd Ave NW	206-783-2262
Scooter's	Burgers, Sandwiches	5802 24th Ave NW	206-782-2966
Shiku	Sushi	5310 Ballard NW	206-588-2151
Snoose Junction	Pizza, Panini	2305 NW Market	206-789-2305
Sunny Teriyaki	Yakisoba, Gyoza	2035 NW Market	206-781-7839
Vera's	Omelets, Sandwiches	5417 22nd Ave NW	206-782-9966
Zak's	Burgers, Salads	2040 NW Market	206-706-9257
Zaw	Artisan Pizza	5458 Leary NW	206-623-0299

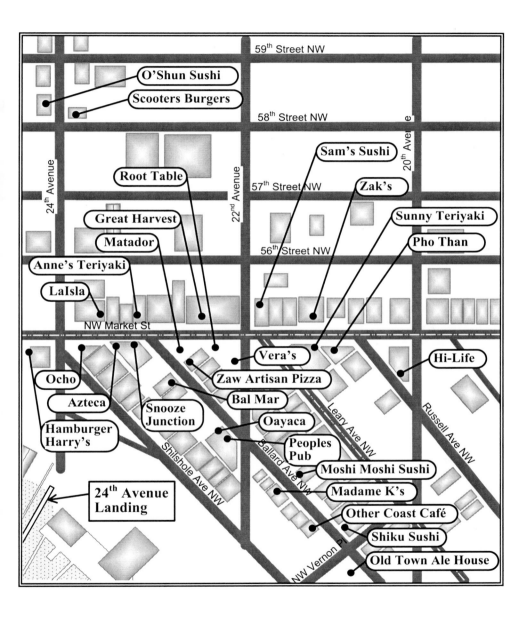

O'Shun Sushi
Scooters Burgers
Sam's Sushi
Zak's
Root Table
Sunny Teriyaki
Great Harvest
Pho Than
Matador
Anne's Teriyaki
LaIsla
Vera's
Hi-Life
Zaw Artisan Pizza
Ocho
Bal Mar
Azteca
Snooze
Junction
Oayaca
Hamburger
Harry's
Peoples
Pub
Moshi Moshi Sushi
24th Avenue
Landing
Madame K's
Other Coast Café
Shiku Sushi
Old Town Ale House

59th Street NW
58th Street NW
57th Street NW
56th Street NW
NW Market St
24th Avenue
22nd Avenue
20th Avenue
Leary Ave NW
Russell Ave NW
Shilshole Ave NW
Ballard Ave NW
NW Vernon Pl

SHIP CANAL
24th Avenue Landing

24TH AVENUE COFFEE & DESSERTS			🍽
Aster Coffee Lounge	Espresso, Quiche, Sandwiches	5615 24th Ave NW	206-784-0615
Café Besalu	Espresso, Pastries	5909 24th Ave NW	206-789-1463
Chai House	Tea, Bagels	5463 Leary Ave NW	206-297-2424
Cugini Café	Coffee, Tea	5306 Ballard Ave NW	206-784-2576
Java Bean	Espresso, Pastries	5819 24th Avenue NW	206-788-9677
Miro Tea	Teas, Sandwiches, Crepes, Pastries	5405 Ballard Ave NW	206-782-6832
Mooberry	Yogurt, Smoothies	2019 NW Market Street	206-706-4842
Starbucks	Espresso, Pastries	2204 NW Market Street	206-782-2795
Tully's	Espresso, Pastries	2060 NW Market Street	206-781-4887
Verite Coffee	Cupcakes, Coffee	2052 NW Market Street	206-782-9557

24TH AVENUE FINE DINING			🍽
Carnegie's	Duck, Lamb, Seafood	2026 NW Market Street	206-789-6643
India Bistro	Indian Cuisine	2301 NW Market Street	206-783-5080
Lombardi's	Pizza, Pasta, Veal	2200 NW Market Street	206-783-0055
Thaiku	Thai Cuisine	5410 Ballard Ave NW	206-706-7807
Volterra	Italian Cuisine	5411 Ballard Ave NW	206-789-5100

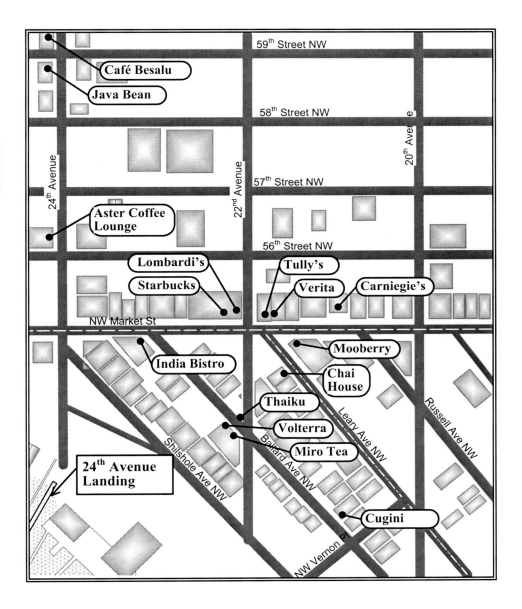

SHIP CANAL
24th Avenue Landing

HI-LIFE 🍽

This unique and fun restaurant housed in the historic 1911 firehouse is located in the heart of Ballard, look for the "Eat-Drink" sign atop the brick building's elevator shaft. The Hi-Life serves wood-fired pizzas, "square meals," and delicious "small plates" like Bread & Cheese trays, Phyllo Prawns, and Roasted Beet Salad; or try the Sicilian olives stuffed with Bleu cheese fried with garlic and sage leaves, or perhaps the slow simmered Oxtail served with Mascarpone polenta and demi glace. Don't forget the great "Tap Beers" to accompany your favorite pizza.

Breakfast/ Lunch	8:30am – 3pm Daily
Dinner	5pm – 10pm Sun-Thur 5pm – 11pm Fri & Sat Bar open till late
Price	Moderate
Outdoor Seating	Yes, Patio, Summer Months
Contact	206-784-7272

"Square Meals" include Roast Chicken, Grilled Wild Salmon, and the wood-grilled Pork Porterhouse, to name a few. Come join the "Hi-Life" in this old brick firehouse with casual appeal, a full service bar, pizza bar, and ample open-style seating.

MATADOR 🍽

Located in a brick pie-shaped building at the junction of Market & Ballard Ave., this classy 21 and over lounge restaurant sports a wood-inlaid bar, antique light fixtures, custom ironwork, and a cozy open fire pit where folks gather to meet and greet. During the summer months, you can enjoy sidewalk seating while sipping one of the 70 Tequila varieties and sampling specialty starters like the Spicy Fried Calamari or the Goat Cheese Overstuffed Jalapenos wrapped with hickory smoked bacon.

Lunch/ Dinner	11am – 2am Daily
Price	Moderate
Outdoor Seating	Yes, Sidewalk, Summer Months
Contact	206-297-2855

Entrees include Grilled Prawn Skewers, Habanero Enchiladas, and Halibut with roasted tomatillo tequila salsa; or try the Matador Grilled Rib-eye, topped with chipotle butter and served with "garlic mashers" and seasonal vegetables. For a lighter fare, try the Spinach Pear Salad and the Roasted Tomato Chicken Soup.

SHIP CANAL
24th Avenue Landing

ROOT TABLE 🍽

The Root Table is a fitting name for this restaurant with its unusual wood tables and chairs made from tree knots, roots, and other natural wood pieces. The menu incorporates natural fruits, vegetables, and spices in sandwiches, tapas, and entrees like the Coriander Kebobs, served with papaya salad and jasmine rice; or try the Double-Fisted Duck, marinated in dark beer served with deep-fried cabbage.

Lunch/ Dinner	11:30am – 11pm Daily
Price	Moderate
Outdoor Seating	No
Contact	206-420-3214

Tapas like Root Fries (seasoned vegetable fries), Lemongrass Chicken, and the Grilled Prawns & Asian Pesto create a nice lunch; or choose one of the sandwiches like the Curry Chicken or the meat Satay with cucumber, red onion, and spicy peanut sauce. Don't forget to finish with a nice Mango Cheesecake.

VOLTERRA

The Volterra restaurant located in "Old Ballard" is a true gem offering contemporary Italian fare. The restaurant is named after the hill-top city of Volterra in Tuscany, where Chef Curtiss found inspiration for his menu. The restaurant is adorned with beautiful sconces and alabaster light fixtures created by artisans in Volterra, which complement the red walls, warm woods, and tile floors. The menu is equally pleasing with Bruschetta, Assorted Cured Meats, and Antipasti for starters followed by the Roasted Beet & Arugula Salad among other delightful selections.

Dinner	5pm - 10pm Mon-Thur 5pm – 11pm Fri & Sat 5pm – 9pm Sunday
Brunch	9am – 2pm Sat & Sun
Price	Moderate
Outdoor Seating	Yes, Patio, Summer Months
Contact	206-789-5100

Entrees include the Wild Boar Tenderloin with Gorgonzola sauce served with Yukon Gold potato gratin and seasonal market vegetables; or try the Sautéed Jumbo Prawns or perhaps the Thin Spaghetti & Crab tossed in a spicy tomato sauce. Stop by Volterra for a taste of Tuscany any day of the week or enjoy a special weekend brunch.

ELLIOTT BAY
Bell Harbor Marina

Visiting Seattle by boat is a delight and is a great option for locals wishing to avoid the gridlock found on many surface streets and freeways in this metropolitan area. Bell Harbor Marina, located on Seattle's waterfront, offers hourly and overnight moorage with easy access to restaurants, parks, and museums. Look for the spire sculpture at the Harbor entrance. Hourly rates are $15 for 0-3 hours and $20 for 4-6 hours regardless of boat length, call ahead to check availability. Guests should report to the Office (kiosk) upon arrival to make payment and obtain a gate access code. If arriving after hours use the self-registration payment box at the Office door and see the security guard for the access code. Office hours are 7am to 6pm during the summer months and 7am to 5:30pm in the off-season. Hourly spaces are marked and located along the main breakwater between "B&C" docks, between "A&B" docks, and north of "A" dock. The dock nearest the gangway is reserved for members of the Muckleshoot Nation. Slips for overnight stays may be reserved in advance; rates are based on the season and length of vessel ranging from $1 to $2 per foot, per night. Bell Harbor is a favorite destination for yacht clubs from other locations in Puget Sound, who reserve slips up to two years in advance.

Five restaurants and a Starbucks are all easily accessible from the Marina. Additional restaurants can be found along the waterfront on Alaskan Way, both north and south of the Marina. Locals and tourist alike enjoy the unique shopping located in the warehouses on the piers along the waterfront, which once held cargo off-loaded from sailing vessels in the 1800's. Don't miss Seattle's famous Pike Place Market with its collection of shops, eateries, and fresh fish, meats, cheeses, and produce, which has been in operation for over a 100 years. To access the Market, follow the large set of stairs marked "Pike Place Hill Climb" about three blocks south of the Marina. A visit to the Olympic Sculpture Park provides another opportunity to stretch your legs and enjoy the beautiful views of Elliott Bay and the Olympic Mountains. This nine-acre park, located several blocks north of the Marina, displays a variety of sculptures in an outdoor setting. The Taste Café located in the Park's pavilion offers picnic fare with seating and indoor swings. Additional delights include the Odyssey Maritime Discovery Center (206-374-4000) located adjacent to Bell Harbor Marina offering interesting exhibits and interactive displays. The Seattle Aquarium (206-386-4300), located four blocks south of the Marina is always a favorite.

For a taste of Seattle history, be sure to take in the Underground Tour (206-682-4646) located at 608 First Avenue in Pioneer Square, which can be accessed via taxi or Metro bus (206-553-3000) with regular stops at the Marina. Local boaters often arrive at the Marina to attend Mariner games in Safeco Field (206-346-4001) and the Seattle Seahawks in Qwest Field (888-635-4295) located south of Pioneer Square. First-time visitors to Seattle won't want to miss the fabulous views from the Space Needle (206-905-2100) at 400 Broad Street, northeast of the Marina on the grounds of the Pacific Science Center. Boaters find that Bell Harbor Marina provides excellent access to many points of interest, fine dining venues, cafes, coffee shops, and entertainment in the heart of Seattle.

Bell Harbor Marina	206-615-3952 VHF 66A
	Port of Seattle, Pier 66

Port of Seattle Marina with short-term and overnight moorage. Restrooms, showers, pumpout. Power and water at docks.

Short-Term: Hourly rates for short-term stays apply as posted for a maximum of 6 hours regardless of length of vessel, call ahead for availability

Overnight: Reservations are accepted for overnight stays with rates based on the season and length of vessel. 24-hour security.

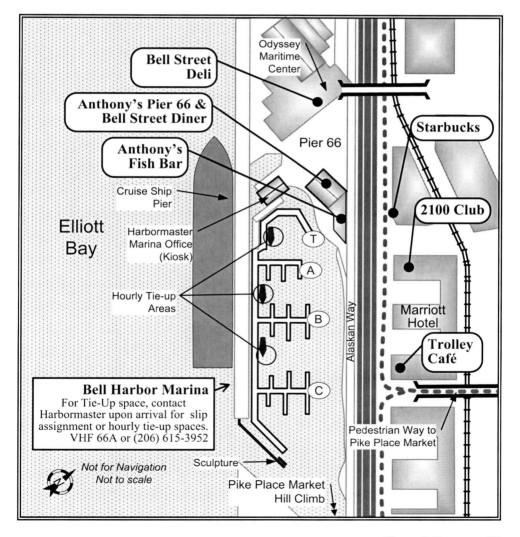

ELLIOTT BAY
Bell Harbor Marina

BELL HARBOR MARINA RESTAURANTS			🍽
Anthony's Pier 66 & Bell Street Diner	Seafood, Steak, Pasta Burgers, Fish	2201 Alaskan	206-448-6688
Anthony's Fish Bar	Fish and Chips	2201 Alaskan	206-448-6688
Bell Street Deli	Groceries, Sandwiches	2207 Alaskan	206-441-6907
2100 Bistro	Seafood, Steak, Sandwiches	2100 Alaskan	206-256-1040
Starbucks	Espresso, Pastries	2200 Alaskan	206-448-9304
Trolley Café	Sandwiches, Soup	2100 Alaskan	206-256-1147

ANTHONY'S PIER 66 & BELL ST. DINER 🍴

Anthony's Pier 66 serves fresh seasonal Northwest seafood dishes and is one of the most chic of Anthony's 20 waterfront locations in the greater Puget Sound area. Dungeness Crab is a highlight, including the crab cocktail, crab chowder, and crab salad. The "Potlatch" is a favorite with steamed clams, fresh local mussels, split steamed Alaskan crab legs, and fresh oysters on the half shell. The contemporary, sophisticated setting upstairs has a commanding view of the Seattle skyline, Mount Rainier, the Olympics and Elliott Bay. Anthony's high-energy Bell Street Diner downstairs features salmon burgers and char-grilled fish on the all-day menu. Local produce and Northwest wines and microbrew complete the fresh Northwest experience.

Lunch	11am – 3pm Daily
Dinner Downstairs	3pm-10pm Mon-Thur 3pm- 10:30pm Fri & Sat 3pm – 9pm Sundays
Dinner Upstairs	5pm – 9:30pm Mon-Thur 5pm – 10pm Fri & Sat 5pm – 9pm Sundays
Price	Moderate - Expensive
Outdoor Seating	Yes, Deck, Summer Months
Contact	206-448-6688

2100 BISTRO 🍴

The 2100 Bistro is located in the elegant Marriott Hotel. The spacious dining room and bar has a classy cosmopolitan appeal with its modern décor and tile floors. The Bistro serves regional and organic foods like Penn Cove Mussels and the Organic Greens Salad. The Dungeness Crab in red wine béarnaise, served with tarragon potatoes is a house favorite. Be sure to ask about the Seasonal Catch served with fresh vegetables or inquire with your server about the Butcher's Cut. For a more casual fare, you can order panini, soups, burgers, or pizza for lunch along with house sides.

Lunch Bar	11am – 11pm Daily
Dinner	5pm – 9pm Daily
Price	Moderate - Expensive
Outdoor Seating	No
Contact	206-256-1040

ELLIOTT BAY
Elliott Bay Marina

One of the largest marinas in the Seattle area, Elliott Bay Marina offers 1,200 slips ranging in size from 32 feet to 63 feet with dock ends that can accommodate most any sized pleasure craft. There are two great restaurant venues just upland from the docks with beautiful views across the Bay of the Seattle skyline.

To secure a space at the Marina for dining purposes, call the Marina ahead of your expected arrival time and you will be assigned a slip or directed to an available side-tie. After disembarking, check in at the Marina Office located below the Palisade Restaurant to pay the moorage fee of $5 for 3 hours ($10 for vessels over 64 feet) and to obtain an access code for the security gate. The Marina Office is open from 7:30am to midnight. The Harbor Master can be reached after hours by calling the number posted at the Marina.

Rates for extended stays and overnight stays run $1.25 per foot ($1.50 for vessels over 64 feet) and are on a first come, first serve basis, call ahead for availability. Slip pump-out facilities are available on docks A-J.

The cove just east of the Marina is known as Smith Cove and once handled cargo from the rich silk trade with Asia as well as immigration from Japan. Henry Smith, a physician, botanist, farmer, and later a territorial legislator, came west in 1851. He staked a land claim of 160 acres in this deep water cove on Elliott Bay's north side and eventually made a handsome profit when the Great Northern Railway reached Seattle. The silk trade ended around 1942 when nylon was introduced and the U.S. Navy began using the Cove during WWII and through the Korean War. Today, Smith Cove is part of the Port of Seattle and is the terminal for auto imports. Boaters with bikes aboard their vessel can enjoy the bike path around Smith Cove heading southeast to Seattle's main waterfront or north through the train yard to Fishermen's Terminal on the Ship Canal.

Elliott Bay Marina	206-285-4817	VHF 78A
www.elliottbaymarina.net	206-282-8424 Fuel	

A full service marina offering short-term and overnight stays in unoccupied slips and side-tie spaces. Restrooms, showers, and laundry. Power, water, and pump-out at docks. Fuel at G-dock with mini-mart, 24-hour security.

Short-Term: Maximum 3 hour stay with fee, call ahead for availability.

Overnight: Overnight stays with fees ranging from $1.25-$1.50 per foot, call ahead for availability, first come, first serve.

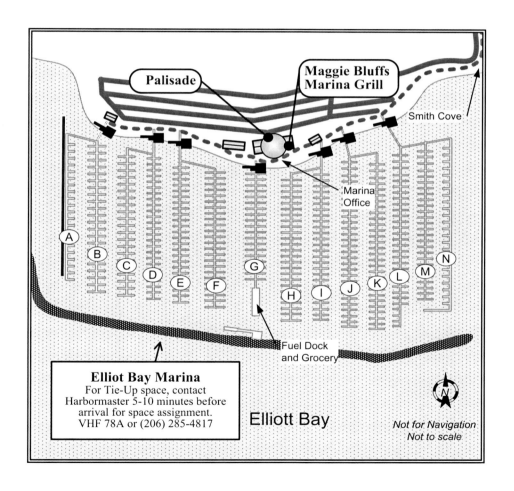

Palisade

Maggie Bluffs Marina Grill

Smith Cove

Marina Office

Fuel Dock and Grocery

Elliot Bay Marina
For Tie-Up space, contact Harbormaster 5-10 minutes before arrival for space assignment.
VHF 78A or (206) 285-4817

Elliott Bay

Not for Navigation
Not to scale

ELLIOTT BAY
Elliott Bay Marina

MAGGIE BLUFF'S MARINA GRILL

This cozy, casual café with wood paneling and tile and wood floors is an intimate, friendly café that is popular among the locals. The view is superb, looking southeast across Elliott Bay toward the Space Needle and the Seattle skyline. The menu is varied and includes a wide selection of sandwiches, burgers, and garden salads. Try the Crisp Greens Salad with creamy blue cheese, toasted almonds, hard-cooked egg, and sweet bay shrimp. On colder days, enjoy the prime rib chili or the grill clam chowder, or perhaps one of the hearty noodle dishes like the Salmon Soba. The full-service bar offers onion rings, shoestring fries, chicken wings, and other "finger food for friends."

Breakfast	9am – 11:30am Sat & Sun
Lunch/ Dinner	11am – 9pm Mon-Thur 11am – 9:30pm Fri & Sat Sunday Summers Hrs. Vary Seasonally
Price	Moderate
Outdoor Seating	Yes, Patio, Summer Months
Contact	206-283-8322

PALISADE 🍽

The Palisade Restaurant is located above the Marina Office and has a panoramic view of downtown Seattle, the Space Needle, Mount Rainier, and the Olympic Mountains not to mention all the boating activity of Elliott Bay. Getting to your table can be an adventure in itself as you cross a bridge suspended over a saltwater tide pool with live fish. The warm woods add to the nautical feel of this spacious restaurant, which includes a large bar that stays open 2 hours after the last dinner seating. The Palisade features fresh seafood cuisine combining Pacific and Polynesian influences along with steak, duck, and chicken selections.

Lunch	11:15am – 2pm Mon-Fri
Dinner	5pm – 9pm Mon-Thur 5pm – 10pm Fridays 4pm – 10pm Saturdays 4pm – 9pm Sundays
Brunch	9:30am – 2pm Sundays
Price	Expensive
Outdoor Seating	Yes, Deck, Summer Months
Contact	206-285-1000

Live crab, lobster, cedar plank salmon, prime rib, and other dishes are prepared in specialty ovens and grills. Desserts include the Polynesian chocolate fondue, seasonal fruit crisp, and the spiced banana ice cream sundae.

ELLIOTT BAY
Seacrest Park

This City of Seattle dock and park possess the most stupendous view of the Seattle skyline, including the Cascade Mountains, Mt. Rainier, Mt. Baker, and the marine activity of Elliott Bay.

An L-shaped floating dock located on the southwest side of a high fishing pier offers boaters tie-up space on the inside of the float. The base of the L-shaped float is reserved for boats rented through the Alki Crab & Fish Company. The south end, outside of the L-float is reserved for the Elliott Bay Water Taxi (206-205-3866), which is operated by King Co. Metro and runs April to Labor Day. Both reserved areas are marked on the float/dock. The remainder of the float is available as guest space for boaters up to 2 hours. This fact often goes unnoticed even by local boaters who are lead to believe the space is for loading and unloading purposes. The float is removed during the winter months and is normally available for use May through September or until early October. Seacrest Park and the surrounding area is a popular scuba diving location and the fishing pier is populated with pole & line folks so be careful when arriving and departing.

Two restaurants and the Bubbles coffee/tea shop are within easy walking distance of Seacrest Park or you can pack a lunch and enjoy the walking paths and picnic tables along the shoreline.

SEACREST PARK RESTAURANTS			🍽
Alki Crab & Fish	Fish Baskets	1660 Harbor Ave	206-938-0975
Bubbles	Espresso, Teas	1619 Harbor Ave	206-938-0153
Salty's	Seafood, Steak, Pasta	1936 Harbor Ave	206-937-1600

Boaters with bikes can easily access additional restaurants in the west Seattle community of Alki Point by heading northwest along the promenade. Alki offers beautiful sandy beaches and many interesting cafes.

Alki Beach is the site where the schooner Exact landed with the Denny Party in 1851 with some of Seattle's first permanent European settlers. The approximate landing site is marked by the Alki Pylon at the foot of 63rd Ave. SW & Alki Ave. SW and lists members of the Denny Party. To learn more about the birthplace of Seattle and the Duwamish Peninsula, visit The Log House Museum (206-938-5293) located one block south of Alki Beach at 3003 61st Ave. SW, the Museum is housed in a restored 1904 log building. Lighthouse enthusiasts will want to visit the Alki Point Lighthouse built in 1913 located at the west end of Alki Avenue. Tours are available on the weekends during the summer months. Contact information and hours are posted at the Lighthouse.

Seacrest Park Dock

206-684-4075
Seattle Parks Department

City of Seattle public float with approximately 100 feet of side-tie available May through September. No power or water at float/dock. Boat launch nearby.

Short-Term: Maximum 2 hour stay at no charge located shore-side of float.
Overnight: No overnight stays.

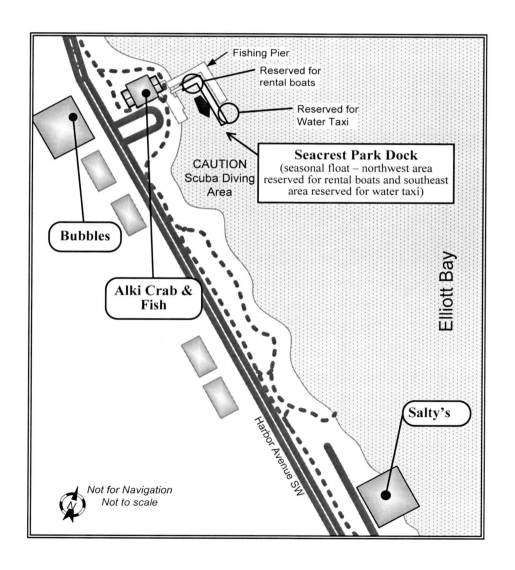

Fishing Pier

Reserved for rental boats

Reserved for Water Taxi

Seacrest Park Dock
(seasonal float – northwest area reserved for rental boats and southeast area reserved for water taxi)

CAUTION
Scuba Diving
Area

Bubbles

Alki Crab & Fish

Elliott Bay

Harbor Avenue SW

Salty's

Not for Navigation
Not to scale

ELLIOTT BAY
Seacrest Park

ALKI CRAB & FISH CO.

The Alki Crab & Fish Co. is a great place to relax with some good fish 'n chips, shrimp and crab cocktails, or a platter of oysters, scallops, and prawns while enjoying the majestic views of the Seattle skyline and the mountains beyond. Be sure to ask about the Manila Clams available in season. This small country style café has cozy indoor seating or you can enjoy an outdoor table on the Café's patio. Bicycles and inline skates are available through the Alki Crab & Fish Co. rental shop during the summer months, call 206-953-0237 for hours and reservations.

Lunch/ Dinner	9am – 8pm Daily Hrs. Extended in Summers
Price	Moderate
Outdoor Seating	Yes, Patio, Summer Months
Contact	206-938-0975

ELLIOTT BAY
Seacrest Park

SALTY'S

Salty's is located just south of Seacrest Park and commands the same incredible panoramic view as does the Park. This restaurant has plenty of windows, patios, and decks from which to observe the ferry traffic, the barges and tugs, freighters, and pleasure boats. Salty's completes the ambiance with its nautical décor of fishing rods and a cozy fireplace. The extensive menu includes salmon, oysters, clams, prawns, and live crab and lobster. Additional choices include pasta, chicken, and char-broiled steaks. Friday and Monday nights at Salty's are especially fun with live jazz entertainment. The Brunch buffet is outstanding and includes a variety of meats, seafood, fruits, crepes, omelets, and Eggs Benedict just to name a few of the many choices. Salty's has been a Seattle icon for many years and continues to maintain its popularity with locals and tourists alike.

Lunch	11am – 3pm Mon-Fri
Dinner	5pm – 10pm Mon-Thur 5pm – 10:30pm Fridays 4pm – 10:30pm Sat 4pm – 10 pm Sundays Winter Hours Vary
Brunch	9am – 1:30pm Sat & Sun
Price	Moderate - Expensive
Outdoor Seating	Yes, Deck(s) Summer Months
Contact	206-937-1600

SHILSHOLE BAY
Shilshole Marina

Shilshole Bay Marina, located just west of the Hiram M. Chittenden Locks, is the largest marina in the Seattle area and just recently completed a three-year renewal and dock replacement project to accommodate kayaks to mega-yachts. Transient guest moorage is available in unoccupied slips in addition to 200 feet of side-tie on 'W' Pier and 350 feet of side-tie on 'H' Pier along with (18) 50-foot slips. The fuel dock is located on the end of 'H' Pier and is open daily from 8am to 6pm during the summer months. Short-term stays up to 6 hours are .25/foot and are first come, first serve; captains should call at the breakwater to be directed to a slip or side-tie. Reservations are accepted for stays over 6 hours, rates vary depending on length of vessel and season ranging from .85/foot to $1.50/foot as posted at the Marina Office located upland. If arriving after hours, use the self-registration payment box outside the office door, or call the after-hours number for assistance. Office hours are 8am to 4:30pm Mon-Sat and closed on Sundays. The beautiful new office building showcases outdoor art and a children's play fountain.

Located south of the Marina at 6135 Seaview Ave. NW is Anthony's HomePort restaurant and is within walking distance of the Marina as is Ray's Boathouse & Café. Don't miss the Purple Cow along the way, offering soups, sandwiches, and the famous purple cow shake made from blueberries, cranberries, and strawberries. Located across the street from the Purple Cow is Paseo, a Caribbean take-out joint which has become quite popular. For picnic style burgers and hotdogs, visit Little Coney located on the north end of Shilshole Bay Marina next to the Eddie Vine Boat Ramp.

Be sure to visit the beautiful sandy beaches at Golden Gardens Park just north of the boat ramp with its expansive views of Puget Sound and the renovated 1929 Bathhouse. The growth of Ballard and Seattle in the 1920's and 30's created the demand for a bathhouse at this popular park, which continues to be enjoyed and loved by local citizens. The Bathhouse can be rented for special events and seats up to 140 guests. For Bathhouse reservation information call 206-684-7254 or go to www.seattle.gov/parks/Reservations/GoldenGardens.htm

Shilshole Bay Marina	206-728-3006 VHF 17	
206-783-7555 Fuel	206-601-4089 After Hours	

Port of Seattle marina with short-term and overnight stays. Restrooms, showers, laundry. Power and water at docks, 24-hour security. Fuel with mini-mart and pumpout on 'H' Pier. Launch ramp at north end of marina.

Short-Term:	Short term stays with fee; first come, first serve basis, call ahead for space assignment.
Overnight:	Reservations accepted for overnight stays, rates vary per season and length of vessel. Report to office or use self-registration payment box at office building.

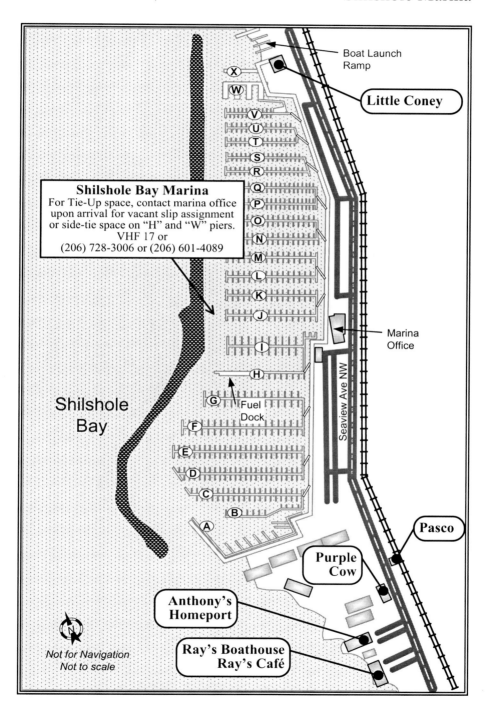

Boat Launch Ramp

Little Coney

Shilshole Bay Marina
For Tie-Up space, contact marina office upon arrival for vacant slip assignment or side-tie space on "H" and "W" piers.
VHF 17 or
(206) 728-3006 or (206) 601-4089

Marina Office

Shilshole Bay

Seaview Ave NW

Fuel Dock

Pasco

Purple Cow

Anthony's Homeport

Ray's Boathouse Ray's Café

Not for Navigation
Not to scale

SHILSHOLE BAY
Shilshole Marina

SHILSHOLE BAY RESTAURANTS			🍽
Anthony's Homeport	Seafood, Steak	6135 Seaview Ave	206-783-0780
Little Coney	Burgers, Hotdogs	8003 Seaview Ave	206-782-6598
Paseo	Caribbean To-Go	6226 NW Seaview	206-789-3100
Ray's Boathouse **Ray's Cafe**	Seafood, Steak, Burgers, Fish, Beer	6049 Seaview Ave 6049 Seaview Ave	206-789-3770 206-782-0094
The Purple Cow	Sandwiches, Pastries, Smoothies	6301 Seaview Ave	206-784-1417

PASEO		🍽
Paseo is located less than a quarter mile south of Shilshole Bay Marina on Seaview Avenue; look for the hot-pink building with the large take-out windows. Paseo has become a popular stop for spicy Caribbean fare, including grilled sandwiches like the Cuban Roast made with succulent slow roasted pork in marinade, served with jalapenos; or try the Grilled Chicken Breast, or perhaps the Fresh Fish seared in extra virgin olive oil & garlic tapenade. Other Paseo favorites include the Rice Bean Salad served with jasmine rice, black beans, and seasoned corn on the cob.	Lunch/ Dinner	11am – 8pm Tue-Sat Closed Sun & Mon
	Price	Moderate
	Outdoor Seating	Yes, Picnic Tables, Summer Months
	Contact	206-789-3100

RAY'S BOATHOUSE & CAFE 🍽

Ray's is located one-quarter mile south of Shilshole Bay Marina on Seaview Avenue. This restaurant and café is named after Ray Lichtenberger, who located his boat rental and bait house on this site in 1939, and in 1945 added a coffee house. Ray's has long been a Seattle icon and boaters are very familiar with Ray's 1952 red neon sign seen west of the Locks. Beautiful views of Puget Sound and the Olympic Mountains can be enjoyed from both the Boathouse dining room downstairs, and the more casual Café with its outdoor deck upstairs. Ray's has received high marks in Gourmet Magazine and Food & Wine. Award winning wines are available in more than 400 varieties. The Café offers 20 microbrews and hard-to-get classic European-style beers.

Lunch Café	11:30am – 9:30pm Sun-Thur 11:30am – 10pm Fri & Sat
Dinner Boathouse	5pm – 9pm Sun – Thur 5pm – 9:30pm Fri & Sat
Price	Moderate – Cafe Expensive - Boathouse
Outdoor Seating	Yes, Deck, Summer Months
Contact	206-782-0094 Cafe 206-789-3770 Boathouse 206-789-6309 Catering

Boathouse classic menu items include wood smoked Black Cod, Prawns split and baked in hazelnut-coriander butter, and the grilled Alaskan Halibut with herb potatoes and Savoy cabbage to name just a few. The Café offers dishes like Red Rockfish served with polenta, grilled Salmon Burger, and Crab and Shrimp Cakes.

Blake Island **109**
Blake Island Marine Park 109

Brownsville **113**
Brownsville Marina 113

Dyes Inlet **115**
Silverdale Guest Dock 115

Eagle Harbor **121**
Bainbridge 121

Keyport **133**
Port of Keyport 133

Liberty Bay **137**
Port of Poulsbo 137

Manchester **143**
Manchester Dock 143

Port Madison **147**
Indianola Dock.. 147
Suquamish 149

Sinclair Inlet **153**
Sinclair Inlet Area.. 153
Boat Shed.. 155
Port of Bremerton Marina.................................... 159
Port Orchard Marina & Pier................................. 167

Central Sound

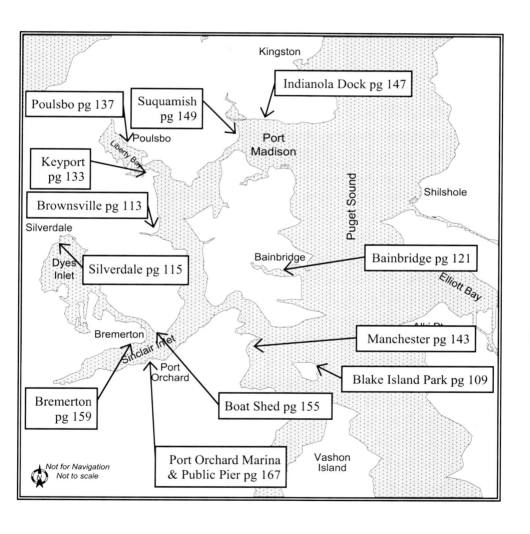

Kingston

Indianola Dock pg 147

Poulsbo pg 137

Suquamish pg 149

Poulsbo

Liberty Bay

Port Madison

Keyport pg 133

Brownsville pg 113

Silverdale

Puget Sound

Shilshole

Dyes Inlet

Silverdale pg 115

Bainbridge

Bainbridge pg 121

Elliott Bay

Bremerton

Sinclair Inlet

Alki Pt

Manchester pg 143

Port Orchard

Blake Island Park pg 109

Bremerton pg 159

Boat Shed pg 155

Port Orchard Marina & Public Pier pg 167

Vashon Island

Not for Navigation
Not to scale

BLAKE ISLAND
Blake Island Marine Park

Blake Island is located southwest of Seattle between Bainbridge and Vashon Islands. Moorage at the Marina is located behind a breakwater on the northeast shore through a marked channel. The first two docks you come to are reserved for tour boats from Seattle and for the State Parks boat. The remaining docks are on a first come, first serve basis for boaters visiting the Island as are the buoys around the Island. Future plans include adding power to the docks and installing additional buoys. A concession stand/window operates May through September and is generally open from 9am to 3pm daily for breakfast items, sandwiches, drinks, and snacks.

Blake Island is best known for its Northwest Coast Indian salmon dinners and native dance performances presented at the Tillicum Village Longhouse, open year-round. It is best to call ahead (206-933-8600) to confirm the dinner hour as times and days vary seasonally and hours are also dependent on tour boat scheduling. Folks arriving by private boat should purchase their tickets at the gift shop an hour ahead of the dinner/performance. Performances include songs and dances portraying stories dealing with nature and creation. During the performance, visitors enjoy a delicious smoked salmon dinner. The salmon is prepared on cedar stakes and cooked over an open fire pit in the Northwest Coast tradition. Blake Island was once the ancestral camping ground of the Suquamish people and legend has it that Chief Selth (Chief Seattle) was born here.

Barbeque pits and picnic tables are available in the marine park along with camp sites and hiking trails throughout the Island. While exploring the Island, don't miss seeing the remains (foundation) of the historic Trimble homestead located just southwest of the Tillicum Village Longhouse. William Trimble and his wife Cassandra and their children lived on the Island from 1917 to 1923. Sadly, Cassandra drowned when their automobile went off the King Street Pier into Elliott Bay. William Trimble never returned to the Island. In 1959, the Washington State Board of Natural Resources set aside all of Blake Island for a marine park.

Blake Island Marine Park   360-731-8330

State Park marina with approximately 1500 feet of dock space. Restrooms, power, and water on shore. No water at docks. Docks and buoys are first come, first serve. Pumpout. Ranger on-site.

Short-Term: Day moorage after 1pm is .50 per foot, minimum $10 charge. Use self-registration payment station upland.

Overnight: Overnight stays after 1pm are .50 per foot with a 7-day limit; Power $6; 24 mooring buoys at $10 a night. Use self-registration payment station at docks.

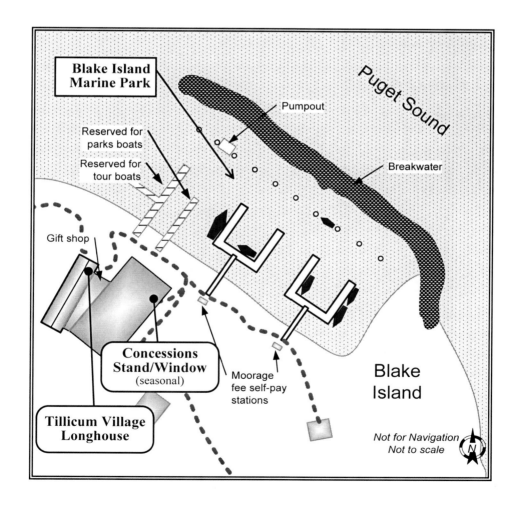

BLAKE ISLAND
Blake Island Marine Park

TILLICUM VILLAGE LONGHOUSE 🍽️

Dining at Tillicum Village is a real treat for both the performance presented in Native dress, including wood-carved head dresses and for the delicious smoked salmon dinner. The meal begins outside the Longhouse with a pot of steamed clams as appetizers. Tradition is to toss the empty shells on the ground and crush them underfoot, thus the pretty white clam shell pathways. Inside the Longhouse, salmon is smoked over an open fire pit of alder around which the salmon is placed on cedar stakes, the aroma and taste is truly a Northwest Coast experience.

Lunch/ Dinner	12:30pm & 5:30pm Daily July – August Days and Hours Vary Off Season
Price	Moderate Show and Dinner
Outdoor Seating	N/A
Contact	206-933-8600

Served buffet style, dinners include new red potatoes, fresh salad, seasonal rice, and delicious dark bread. Coffee and water are available at the tables and guests have the option to purchase select Washington State wines. Tillicum Village is a family owned business begun by the Hewitt family in 1962, who continue to share their love of this special place and the Northwest Coast arts.

BROWNSVILLE
Brownsville Marina

The Port of Brownsville is one of Puget Sound's destination secrets located in Burke Bay behind Bainbridge Island on the western bank of the Port Orchard waterway. This friendly marina situated in a rural setting, offers all the necessary amenities with ample transient moorage on the inside of both the North Breakwater and East Breakwater for large vessels and 25 boat slips for smaller craft located on the west side of 'A' Dock. Guest space is on a first come, first serve basis with the first 4 hours of moorage at no charge. Stays over four hours are .50 per foot and payable at the Port Office located above the Brownsville Marine & Deli or use the self-registration envelope and payment drop at the Port Office door. Office hours are 8am to 8pm daily during the summers and 8am to 5pm winter months. Brownsville is a popular rendezvous destination for clubs, who can make prior reservations for their group at three special event venues: The Yacht Club room above the Deli; the Overlook Park & Gazebo; and the Waterfront Pavilion. Be sure to read the placards in the Pavilion showcasing the area's colorful history.

The Marine & Deli carries grocery items, marine supplies, gifts, and houses a deli with indoor and outdoor seating. For a broader selection of groceries, visit the Daily Stop Grocery (360-692-2073) at the corner of Illahee Rd. and Brownsville Hwy just upland from the Marine & Deli. Don't miss Sweeny's Country Style Meat Co. (360-692-8802) located across the street from the Daily Stop Grocery. Sweeny's is the perfect place to purchase smoked meats to take back to the boat, including smoked bacon, pork chops, ham hocks, and smoked seafood. Venison, German and Polish sausages, and beef ribs are also available.

The area was first homesteaded in the mid 1800's by Scandinavians. Brownsville received excellent ferry service in the early days, which brought visitors to the David Carey Smith Inn that once stood here. The Brownsville dock was built in 1901 by community volunteers and maintained by these folks until 1920 when the Brownsville Port District was formed.

BROWNSVILLE MARINE & DELI

The Deli is located in the Marine & Deli shop with bar-style tables and chairs set among the store's gift items and stocked goods. Orders for fresh salads and custom made sandwiches are taken at the deli bar with your choice of meats, cheeses, and breads. Hot items include the Club Sandwich, the Rueben, and the French Dip along with daily soups. You can even grill your own steak and burgers on the Deli's outdoor patio grill and create your own picnic lunch or dinner with your meat purchases from the Deli. Breakfast items, including English muffins, bagels, and sausages are available during the morning hours.

Breakfast/ Lunch/ Dinner	8am – 8pm Mon-Thur 8am – 9pm Fridays 8am – 8pm Saturdays 8am – 6pm Sundays Closed Mon Off Season
Price	Moderate
Outdoor Seating	Yes, Patio, Enclosed Off Season
Contact	360-692-4127

Brownsville Marina www.portofbrownsville.org	360-692-5498 VHF16/66A 360-692-0687 Fuel Dock

Port of Brownsville marina with short-term and overnight guest moorage with 25 small slips and 1300 feet of side-tie. Pumpout, restrooms, showers, laundry, wheelchair accessible. Power and water at docks. Fuel and launch ramp.

Short-Term: Four-hour stays at no charge; first come, first serve.

Overnight: Overnight stays at .50 per foot, first come, first serve.

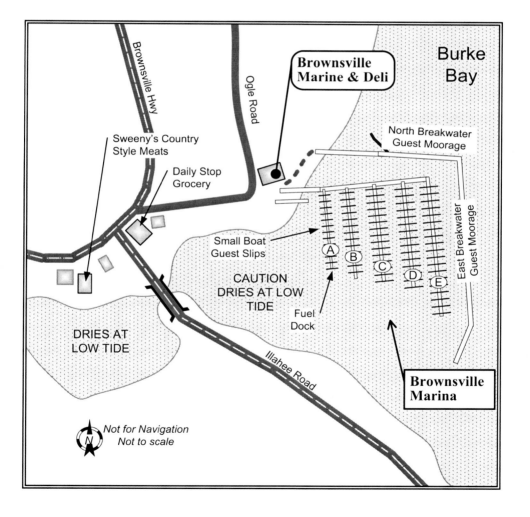

DYES INLET
Silverdale Guest Dock

There is something intriguing about cruising to Silverdale, perhaps it's the passage through Washington Narrows leading into the large bay of water called Dyes Inlet, or perhaps it's the pretty Silverdale Waterfront Park and the village appeal of Old Town Silverdale. The nice public dock, managed by the Port of Silverdale, offers 1300 feet of side-tie for day usage at no charge. Overnight use fees are currently $10/night for boats under 28 feet and $20/night for boats 28 feet and over with a maximum stay of three consecutive nights; use the self-registration payment box at the head of the ramp. Reservations are taken on-line for 5 or more boats.

The attractive Waterfront Park has picnic tables, barbeque pits, a pavilion, and fun play structures for children. Shops and eateries in Old Town Silverdale are within a short walk of the park, including coffee shops, a bakery, cafes, a wine shop, and a bistro night club. You will find the Yacht Club Broiler a few blocks north on the waterfront. Don't miss visiting the community Rose Garden next to the "Knit N Stitch" shop at 3382 Carlton Street. Another must see is the adorable McGregor & Co. shop selling house wares and espresso located on Lowell Street. For personal pampering, visit the BayShore Day Spa (360-698-7721) located next to the Yacht Club Broiler in a cute seaside house.

Events in Old Town Silverdale include the Annual Whaling Days, a popular community event held on the last weekend in July at the Silverdale Waterfront Park. The festivities start on Friday with the Street Fair and evening fireworks followed by a Saturday morning pancake breakfast and parade. Live music, food, and a variety of races, including the outrigger canoe races are all a part of the Whaling Days festivities. Another popular event is the Unlimited Light Hydroplane Races (425-923-5832) or www.ulhra.org, which takes place on Dyes Inlet in August; dates vary depending on the tides. During the weekend race, the Port of Silverdale public dock is closed to boat traffic, but prior reservations for space at the dock can be made through the Unlimited Light Hydroplane Association. Boaters are permitted to anchor on the southeast side of the race course. The one and a quarter mile race course runs in front of the Silverdale Waterfront Park from east to west in an oval shape. Race times vary throughout the weekend with the last race on Sunday.

The first non-natives to settle in Silverdale were loggers in the 1850's. After deforestation in the valley, many farmers came to the area to raise chickens and establish dairy farms. By the early 1900's milk, chicken, and egg production were major industries and the steamer sloop "Telka" made trips to Seattle once a week with passengers and goods. Dyes Inlet takes its name from the assistant taxidermist for Captain Wilkes of the U.S. Navy, who sailed into the bay in 1841.

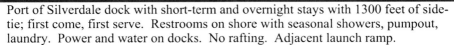

Silverdale Guest Dock 360-698-4918
www.portofsilverdale.com

Port of Silverdale dock with short-term and overnight stays with 1300 feet of side-tie; first come, first serve. Restrooms on shore with seasonal showers, pumpout, laundry. Power and water on docks. No rafting. Adjacent launch ramp.

Short-Term: Short-term day usage at no charge.

Overnight: Overnight stays $10/night for under 28' and $20/night for vessels 28' and over, use self-registration payment box at head of ramp. Reservations on-line with fee. Anchorage nearby.

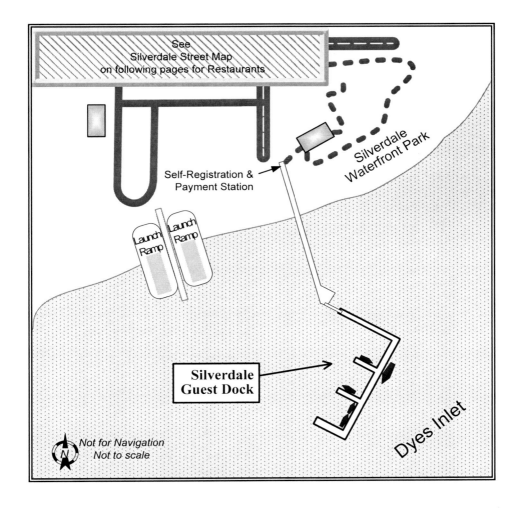

DYES INLET
Silverdale Guest Dock

SILVERDALE OLD TOWN RESTAURANTS 🍽			
Grape Expectations	Wine Shop	3594 NW Byron	360-698-0522
McGregor & Co.	Espresso, Home Gifts	3428 NW Lowell	360-698-5388
Monica's Bakery	Sandwiches, Quiche, Coffee, Baked Goods	3472 NW Byron	360-698-2991
Nattamit	Thai Cuisine	9001 Pacific Ave	360-692-3085
Old Town Bistro	Panini, Salads, Wine Bar, Live Music	3388 NW Byron	360-698-9463
Old Town Flowers	Ice Cream	3343 NW Byron	360-698-0572
Yacht Club Broiler	Burgers, Steak, Seafood, Pasta	9226 Bayshore Drive NW	360-698-1601

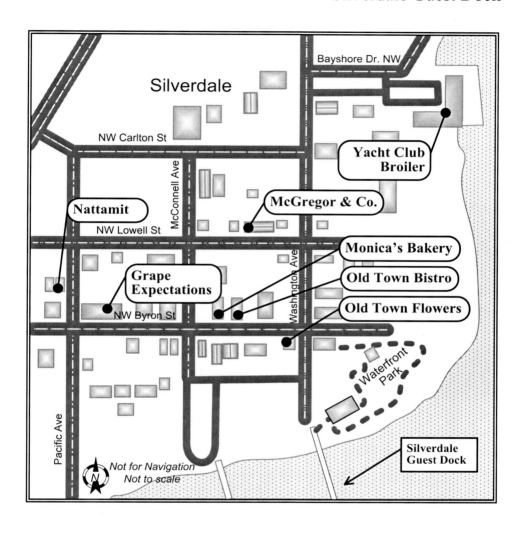

Silverdale

Bayshore Dr. NW

NW Carlton St

McConnell Ave

Yacht Club Broiler

Nattamit

McGregor & Co.

NW Lowell St

Monica's Bakery

Grape Expectations

Old Town Bistro

Washington Ave

Old Town Flowers

NW Byron St

Waterfront Park

Pacific Ave

Not for Navigation
Not to scale

Silverdale Guest Dock

DYES INLET
Silverdale Guest Dock

MONICA'S WATERFRONT BAKERY 🍽

Monica's is a delightful bakery and café with a few tables downstairs and ample seating upstairs. During the summer months, seating extends outdoors on the sidewalk and onto the side deck. Monica's Bakery is the perfect stop for espresso and sweets or for an afternoon lunch, including quiche, house-made soups, and sandwiches created on Monica's freshly made bread. Sandwiches include the Dilled Chicken, the Egg Salad Sandwich, and Betuel's Meatloaf among other choices. Guests can order one of the Gourmet Box Lunches to enjoy at the park or back at the boat, which includes a half-sandwich or wrap, a small salad, fresh fruit, chips, drink, and a cookie.

Hours	7am – 6pm Mon-Fri 8am – 4pm Saturdays
Price	Moderate
Outdoor Seating	Yes, Deck, Summer Months
Contact	360-698-2991

YACH T CLUB BROILER   🍽

To locate the Yacht Club Broiler, walk three blocks north on Washington Avenue and turn right on Bayshore Dr., the Broiler is located on the shoreline. The Yacht Club Broiler offers window-side seating overlooking Dyes Inlet with nautical wood furnishings and linen napkins. The lawn area serves as outdoor seating during the summer months or you can gather with friends in the separate full-service bar to enjoy a wide selection of wine and micro-brews.

Lunch / Dinner	11am – 9pm Mon-Thur 11am – 10pm Fri & Sat 11am – 8pm Sundays
Price	Moderate
Outdoor Seating	Yes, Lawn Area, Summer Months
Contact	360-698-1601

The Broiler offers burgers, sandwiches, pasta, and seafood dishes for lunch with Top Sirloin and New York steaks added to the dinner menu. Seafood dishes include Pacific Salmon and Halibut, Broiled Prawns, Pan Fried Oysters, and Dungeness Crab Cakes among other selections served with steamed vegetables and potatoes. Don't forget dessert like the Coffee Mouse or Apple Pie.

EAGLE HARBOR
Bainbridge

The City of Bainbridge, formerly known as the town of Winslow, is located just 9 miles due west of Seattle in Eagle Harbor, offering several moorage options for visiting boaters. The Waterfront Pack City Dock is located on the north side of Eagle Harbor just west of the ferry landing and ferry maintenance yard. The City's 100 foot dock is first come, first serve and is available up to 3 hours at .10 per foot. Additional hours and overnight stays are .50 per foot; use the self-pay envelopes just upland from the dock. Planned construction to expand the guest dock for additional dinghy dock space will begin in 2010. The City also offers a 200 foot linear buoy system in the middle of the Harbor (flashing amber light at night). The "Harbour Marina," located on the northwest end of the Harbor, offers transient overnight space in unoccupied slips (rates vary) plus a 60 foot 2-hour guest dock (painted blue) for boaters dining at the adjacent Harbor Public House pub and/or Pegasus Coffee House, call ahead prior to arrival for availability. The Winslow Wharf Marina located next door offers overnight transient moorage in unoccupied slips up to 50 feet, reservations are accepted or call ahead between 9am and 5pm during the summer months. Be sure to visit The Chandlery (206-842-7245) just upland on Parfitt Way, which carries marine supplies, books, and nautical gifts. Located on the south side of the Harbor is Eagle Harbor Marina, which may have some transient space available in unoccupied slips, call ahead Tue-Sat from 9am to 5pm for availability.

The City of Bainbridge is filled with wonderful cafes, coffee shops, and restaurants of every kind along with art galleries, gift shops, book stores, and boutiques. Be sure to allow plenty of time to explore this great community. If you have young children, stop by the Kids Discovery Museum (206-855-4650) at 305 Madison Ave., a learning center with fun inter-active games. For a bit of history, visit the Bainbridge Historical Museum (206-842-2773) at 215 Erickson Ave., which is housed in a 1908 school house. The Museum has an excellent map for self-guided walking tours of historic homes and buildings of early Winslow, including photos and commentary. You may want to rent bicycles from Classic Cycle (206-842-3434) at the Bike Barn next to the ferry landing for touring purposes.

The nearby charming village of Lynwood Center is worth a visit for its English Tudor-style buildings and historic theater. Lynwood is located about two and one-half miles from the City of Bainbridge at the crossroads of Lynwood Center Rd. & Pleasant Beach Dr. and is accessible via Bainbridge Island Taxi (206-842-1021) or the Kitsap Transit (800-501-7433) Bus No. 97 and 98. The village offers two good restaurants, the TreeHouse Café (206-842-2814) and Edna's Beach Café (206-842-9690) with beautiful views of Rich Passage.

Early settlers to the area, once called Madrone, arrived in 1878. The name of the town was changed to Winslow in honor of Winslow Hall of the world-famous Hall Brothers Shipyard, which moved from Port Blakely to Eagle Harbor in 1902. The Harbor Public House pub was originally the 1881 home of Amanda and Ambrose Grow, also early settlers of Madrone/Winslow. In 1991 residents voted to change the City's name to Bainbridge after the annexation of the remainder of the Island.

EAGLE HARBOR
Bainbridge

Waterfront Park Dock   206-780-3733
www.ci.bainbridgeisl.wa.us

City of Bainbridge public dock with short-term and overnight stays; first come, first serve on 100 foot dock and 200 foot linear buoy system. Bathrooms and showers. No power or water on dock. Pumpout and launch ramp.

Short-Term: Stays up to 3 hours at .10/ft; space for dinghies with additional space to be added in 2010. Anchorage in Bay.

Overnight: Overnight stays .50/foot, use self-pay envelopes at kiosk upland.

Eagle Harbor Marina   206-842-4003   VHF
www.eagleharbormarina.com

Private marina with limited overnight transient moorage in unoccupied slips up to 66 feet with power and water. Call between 9am and 5pm, Tue-Sat, and again upon arrival. Restrooms, showers, laundry.

Short-Term: No hourly stays.

Overnight: Overnight stays in unoccupied slips at .75 per foot plus power

---

Harbour Marina   206-842-6502
www.parfittway.com   206-550-5340 dockmaster

Private marina with transient space in unoccupied slips with power and water. Restrooms, showers, laundry, and pumpout. Call ahead for availability.

Short-Term: A 60-foot, 2-hour guest dock painted blue for use while dining at the Harbor Public House pub and/or Pegasus Coffee House.

Overnight: Overnight stays in unoccupied slips with fees based on vessel length ranging from $30/night to $45/night power included.

Winslow Wharf Marina   206-842-4202   VHF 09

Private marina with overnight transient moorage in unoccupied slips up to 50 feet with power and water. Restrooms, showers, laundry, pumpout, and Chandlery.

Short-Term: No hourly moorage.

Overnight: Overnight stays $1/foot or slip length whichever is greater. Reservations are accepted. Gate locked at 5pm.

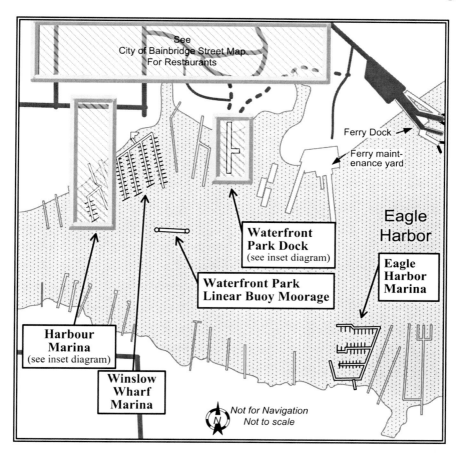

See
City of Bainbridge Street Map
For Restaurants

Ferry Dock

Ferry maintenance yard

Eagle Harbor

Waterfront Park Dock
(see inset diagram)

Eagle Harbor Marina

Waterfront Park Linear Buoy Moorage

Harbour Marina
(see inset diagram)

Winslow Wharf Marina

Not for Navigation
Not to scale

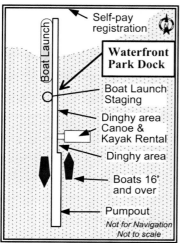

Self-pay registration

Boat Launch

Waterfront Park Dock

Boat Launch Staging

Dinghy area
Canoe & Kayak Rental

Dinghy area

Boats 16' and over

Pumpout

Not for Navigation
Not to scale

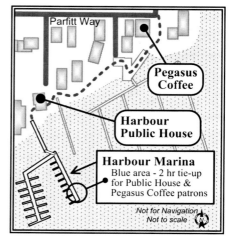

Parfitt Way

Pegasus Coffee

Harbour Public House

Harbour Marina
Blue area - 2 hr tie-up
for Public House &
Pegasus Coffee patrons

Not for Navigation
Not to scale

EAGLE HARBOR
Bainbridge

BAINBRIDGE CITY RESTAURANTS			🍽
Andante Coffee	Espresso, Pastries	123 Bjune Dr.	206-842-1633
Bainbridge Bakers	Panini, Pastries	140 Winslow Wy E	206-842-1822
Bainbridge Is. BBQ	Pork, Ribs, Salmon	251 Winslow Wy W	206-842-7427 (deliveries)
Bainbridge Thai	Thai Cuisine	330 Madison Ave S	206-780-2403
Blackbird Bakery	Espresso, Pastries, Soups, Quiche	210 Winslow Wy E	206-780-1322
Bon Bon	Chocolates, Candy	123 Bjune Dr #103	206-780-0199
Café Nola	Sandwiches, Steak, Seafood, Salads	101 Winslow Wy E	206-842-3822
Café Pavilion	Ice Cream	403 Madison Ave N (Pavilion Center)	206-842-1769
Café Trios	Small Plates, Wine	772 Winslow Wy E	206-842-3986
Casa Rojas	Mexican Cuisine	403 Madison Ave N (Pavilion Center)	206-855-7999
Doc's Marina Grill	Sandwiches, Steak, Pasta, Seafood	403 Madison Ave S	206-842-8339
Eleven Winery	Wine Shop & Taste	278 Winslow Wy E (Winslow Mall)	206-842-4669
Emmy's VegeHouse	Asian Cuisine	100 Winslow Way	206-855-2996 (orders to-go)
Flowering Around	Espresso, Sweets	200 Winslow Wy W	206-842-0620
Four Swallows	Seafood, Beef, Duck, Pizza	481 Madison Ave N	206-842-3397
Gandhi	Indian Cuisine	403 Madison Ave N	206-780-3545
Harbor Public House	Sandwiches, Soup, Burgers, Salads	231 Parfitt Wy SW	206-842-0969
Harbor Square Wine	Wine Shop and Tasting	756 Winslow Wy E	206-780-1626

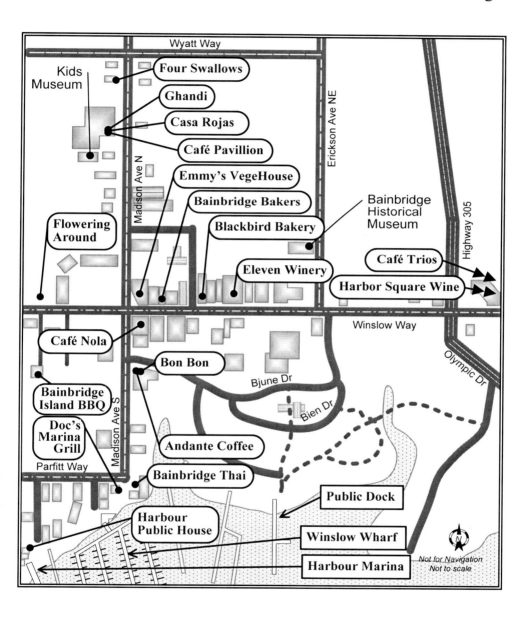

Kids Museum

Four Swallows

Ghandi

Casa Rojas

Café Pavillion

Emmy's VegeHouse

Bainbridge Bakers

Blackbird Bakery

Bainbridge Historical Museum

Flowering Around

Eleven Winery

Café Trios

Harbor Square Wine

Café Nola

Bon Bon

Bainbridge Island BBQ

Doc's Marina Grill

Andante Coffee

Bainbridge Thai

Public Dock

Harbour Public House

Winslow Wharf

Harbour Marina

Wyatt Way

Erickson Ave NE

Madison Ave N

Highway 305

Winslow Way

Olympic Dr

Bjune Dr

Bien Dr

Madison Ave S

Parfitt Way

Not for Navigation
Not to scale

EAGLE HARBOR
Bainbridge

BAINBRIDGE CITY RESTAURANTS			🍽
Isla Bonita	Mexican Cuisine	316 Winslow Wy E	206-780-9644
Madoka	Seafood, Duck, Lamb, Pork	241 Winslow Wy W	206-842-2448
Mon Elisa's	Italian Cuisine (homemade pasta)	450 Winslow Wy E	206-780-3233 (orders to-go)
Mora Iced Creamery	Ice Cream, Sorbet	139 Madrone Ln N	206-855-8822
Pegasus Coffee House	Espresso, Panini, Salads, Desserts	131 Parfitt Way SW	206-842-6725
Real Foods Café (Store & Café)	Sandwiches, Wraps, Soups	764 Winslow Wy E	206-842-3333 206-842-3312
San Carlos	Southwestern	279 Madison Ave N	206-842-1999
Shima Sushi	Japanese Cuisine	112 Madison Ave N	206-855-9400
Simon's	Chinese Cuisine	403 Madison Ave N (Pavilion Center)	206-855-1845
Spice Route	Indian Cuisine	403 Madison Ave	206-780-3545
Streamliner Diner	Breakfast, Soups, Sandwiches	397 Winslow Wy E	206-842-8595
Subway	Sandwiches	278 Winslow Wy E (Winslow Mall)	206-780-5354
Teriyaki Town	Japanese Cuisine	278 Winslow Wy E (Winslow Mall)	206-855-1200
That's A Some Pizza	Pizza, Sandwiches	488 Winslow Wy E	206-842-2292
Town & Country	Groceries, Coffee	343 Winslow Wy E	206-842-3848
Westside Pizza	Take-out Pizzas	278 Winslow Wy E	206-780-0755
122 Dining & Cheer	Seafood, Burgers	122 Winslow Way E	206-842-6122

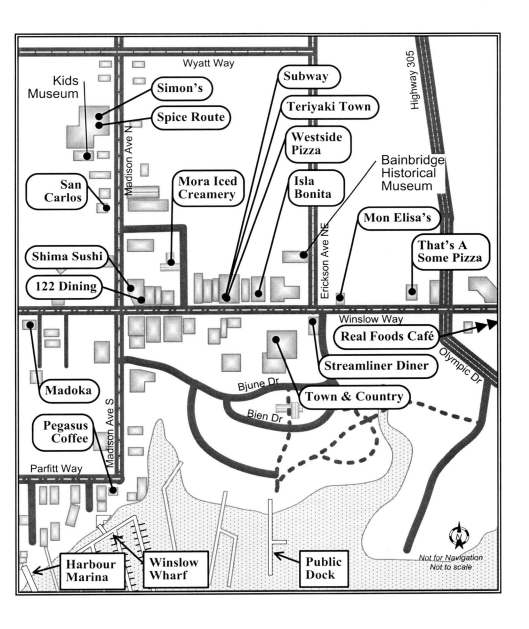

EAGLE HARBOR
Bainbridge

Wyatt Way

Kids Museum

Simon's

Spice Route

Subway

Teriyaki Town

Westside Pizza

Isla Bonita

Bainbridge Historical Museum

Highway 305

San Carlos

Mora Iced Creamery

Mon Elisa's

That's A Some Pizza

Madison Ave N

Erickson Ave NE

Shima Sushi

122 Dining

Winslow Way

Real Foods Café

Streamliner Diner

Olympic Dr

Madoka

Bjune Dr

Town & Country

Bien Dr

Pegasus Coffee

Madison Ave S

Parfitt Way

Harbour Marina

Winslow Wharf

Public Dock

N

Not for Navigation
Not to scale

EAGLE HARBOR
Bainbridge

FOUR SWALLOWS

The Four Swallows restaurant is located in the historic 1889 William Grow House at 481 Madison Avenue. William was the son of Ambrose Grow, who moved his family to Bainbridge from Kansas via rail to San Francisco. William and his brother Frank arrived by ox team across the plains. Today, the home serves as a fine dining venue with formal and casual spaces and a lovely porch for outdoor summer dining.

Dinner	5:30pm – 9pm Tue-Sat Closed Sun & Mon
Price	Moderate - Expensive
Outdoor Seating	Yes, Porch, Summer Months
Contact	206-842-3397

The menu includes seafood, beef, and duck along with an extensive list of fine wines. Tasty dishes include Alaskan Halibut with applewood smoked bacon, roasted white corn, and heirloom tomatoes; or try the Pan Roasted Beef Tenderloin with red wine demi, mashed potatoes, and rainbow chard. Special dinners are announced on occasion like the five-course Italian Wine Dinner, call ahead for schedules and reservations.

SHIMA SUSHI

Shima Sushi is located near the corner of Madison and Winslow accessed via a narrow alley way. Visitors are immediately transported to the old world charm of Japan. Cozy tables for two are separated by cloth panels, or you can sit at the bar and watch the art of preparing sushi. Larger groups will enjoy the back dining room with window views, and bamboo cubicles are available along the alley during the summer months.

Lunch	11:30am – 2pm Mon-Fri
Dinner	5:30pm – 9pm Daily
Price	Moderate
Outdoor Seating	Yes, Alley Way, Summer Months
Contact	206-855-9400

Shima features organic ingredients in its extensive menu. Appetizers include Albacore dipped in ponzu sauce, and the Nasu, an organic eggplant with sweet miso sauce; or perhaps start with a miso soup or the Organic Baked Beets & Organic Greens. Entrees include the sweet marinated Black Cod and the Roasted Natural Chicken with sweet orange sauce. Sushi enthusiast will love the Sashimi, Sushi, and Chirashi dinners followed by the Sweet Plum Wine.

EAGLE HARBOR
Bainbridge

BAINBRIDGE ISLAND BBQ   🍽

The Bainbridge Island Barbeque offers a fun and casual venue for delicious barbeque prepared on-site by the grill-master, including pulled pork, ribs, and salmon offered with homemade sauces like the Whiskey Brown Sugar, the Chipotle Honey, and the Bainbridge Habanero Insane. Guests start off with a complimentary basket of warm roasted peanuts and are invited to throw the shells on the floor, all part of the fun at this barbeque house decorated with hay bales and longhorns.

Breakfast	Holidays
Lunch/ Dinner	11am – 8pm Tue-Sun Closed Mondays
Price	Moderate
Outdoor Seating	Yes, Patio, Summer Months
Contact	206-842-7427

Sandwiches include the BBQ Beef Brisket, and Ian's Prime Rib Dip among other choices. Kids will love the Huge Hot Dog, cowboy style, and the Camper's Smores for dessert. For a complete meal, be sure to order the Sides, including Grandma Ruth's Cole Slaw, Smoky Beans, or the Yukon Gold Potato Salad. A breakfast buffet with an Omelet Bar is available on Saturdays and Sundays. Boaters can place orders for dockside delivery or visit their "serious barbeque" at the end of Winslow Way W. at 251, past the Madoka Pan-Pacific restaurant.

PEGASUS COFFEE HOUSE

The Pegasus Coffee House is located in the historic 1937 Anderson Hardware store, a brick building covered with ivy on Parfitt Way. This cool coffee house offers Island roasted coffee, teas, and pastries along with a Panini Bar for custom made sandwiches. Bruschetta Plates, Small Plates, and Salads are special treats as well at Pegasus. Start your day with an Egg Strata, layers of bread, whipped eggs, and cheese baked with vegetables and meat.

Lunch/ Small Plates	7am – 6pm Mon-Thur 7am – 9:30pm Fri-Sun
Price	Moderate
Outdoor Seating	Yes, Patio, Summer Months
Contact	206-842-6725

Or stop by for lunch to try a custom Panini or the Sliced Meat & Cheese Plate. Bruschetta with savory toppings accompanied with the Organic Greens is a good choice any time of day followed with a sweet pastry and a cup of espresso. Don't miss the lovely patio on the backside of the building, a great place to relax on a sunny day. Music nights are held at the Pegasus on Thursdays, Fridays, and Saturdays with open mic on Sundays. Bottled beers and wine are available for purchase.

KEYPORT
Port of Keyport

Keyport is one of the most unique landings in Puget Sound with two historic restaurants and the nearby Naval Undersea Museum. The small marina at Keyport has five 30ft. slips and a 45 foot public float for guests located just past the Keyport Naval Undersea Warfare Center (NUWC) near the entrance to Liberty Bay. A viable option for larger vessels is to arrive at Keyport via dinghy from Poulsbo. Boaters can tie-up for 6 hours while visiting the Naval Undersea Museum or while dining at the two local restaurants. Current plans include replacing the existing slips in June of 2009 to be made available for overnight stays; fees are yet to be determined. For the latest information, call Port of Keyport.

Visiting the Naval Undersea Museum (360-396-4148) at Keyport is definitely a highlight. This excellent museum features exhibits on the ocean environment and the technologies of diving, submarines, torpedoes, and mine warfare, including a Japanese Kamikaze torpedo, and the Trieste, a submersible that went to the bottom of the Mariana Trench. Not surprising, Keyport's nickname is "Torpedo Town USA" and was one of the filming locations for the 1990 movie, "The Hunt for Red October."Many of the exhibits offer hands-on activities. The Museum is open daily from 10am to 4pm and is closed on Tuesdays during the off season, admission is free. The walk to the Museum from the public float is about one-half mile, follow Washington Ave. NE to Highway 308 and then south to McKittrick Rd., you will see signage for the Museum.

Keyport's early settlers were farmers during the mid to late 1800's who named their community "Keyport." A general store that was built in 1903 was located on the tip of the peninsula where the Naval Undersea Warfare Center is now located. Due to the installation of these facilities, the general store, which became known as the Keyport Mercantile, was moved to its present location on Washington Avenue. Keyport like most other waterfront communities of the time was serviced by the "Mosquito Fleet" steamers, which were active from the 1880's to the early 1920's.

Port of Keyport	360-779-4259	
	Port of Keyport	

Port of Keyport marina with five 30ft. slips and a 45 foot guest dock for visitors. Slips being replaced in June 2009 with same configuration.

Short-Term: Maximum stay of 6 hours at no charge.

Overnight: Overnight stays with fees yet to be determined. Future pay box.

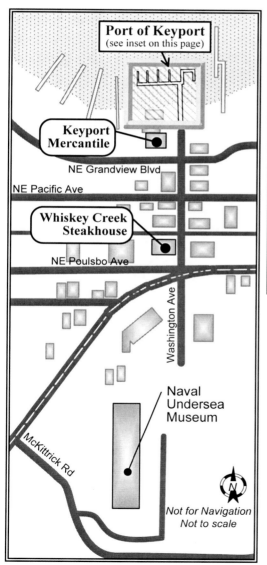

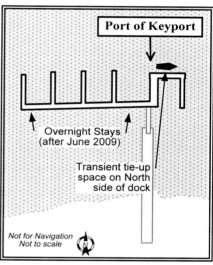

KEYPORT
Port of Keyport

KEYPORT MERCANTILE

The Keyport Mercantile is located upland from the public float at the corner of Washington Ave. NE and NE Grandview Blvd. This adorable grocery store and sandwich shop was built in 1903 and relocated in 1914 from the peninsula to its present location. You can purchase goods for your boat's galley or enjoy a mercantile sandwich like the Dogfish Bay Tuna Salad made with celery and dill relish, or try the Sow's Ear with turkey and roast beef, or perhaps the pastrami. Sandwiches come with your choice of bread, cheese, veggies, and condiments, served with chips, pickle, and choice of potato or corn/bean salad. Seating is available inside the shop with lovely views of Liberty Bay and at umbrella shaded tables outside the Mercantile.

Hours	6am – 9pm Mon-Fri 8am – 9pm Saturday 8am – 8pm Sunday
Price	Moderate
Outdoor Seating	Yes, Sidewalk, Summer Months
Contact	360-779-7270

WHISKEY CREEK STEAKHOUSE

The Whiskey Creek Steakhouse is one of the most fun and unique eateries in Puget Sound. This historic building served as a mercantile in 1927 and became the Keyport Tavern in 1934, later renamed The Torpedo Shop. The current owners transformed the tavern into a fun family restaurant and pub. The rocks in the fireplace are from Whiskey Creek Beach, northwest of Port Angeles. The décor is reminiscent of a rustic mountain cabin with hides, mounts, riding saddles, and other western décor, including the hitching post out front.

Lunch/	11am – 4pm Daily
Dinner	4:30pm – 9:30pm Mon-Sat 4pm – 9pm Sundays Hours Vary Off Season
Price	Moderate
Outdoor Seating	Yes, Patio, Summer Months
Contact	360-779-3481

Old wood floors with lit wood branches overhead give a touch of romance. For more casual seating you can "belly-up" to the bar or enjoy the cute back patio during the summer months. Live piano and bass is held most every night starting at 5pm. As the name implies, you will find quality steaks at the Whiskey Creek Steakhouse ranging in size from the Petite 6oz. New York Strip to the King 18oz. Porterhouse. Other choices include the Prime Rib, Prime Top Sirloin, Rib-eye, and the Filet Mignon along with burgers and seafood selections. Lunch choices include chili, salads, and sandwiches. "To Go" orders are welcome, please call ahead.

LIBERTY BAY
Port of Poulsbo

Poulsbo, known for its Norwegian heritage, is one of Puget Sound's most popular destinations and the Port of Poulsbo Marina can be filled to capacity on busy summer weekends. The Marina is located at the end of the Bay on the north bank and offers 130 guest slips and 3 side-tie spaces for large yachts. 'F' Dock is primarily first come first serve with a maximum of 10 reservations accepted. Yacht clubs can make reservations for 10 or more boats on 'E' Dock. Moorage rates are .85 per foot with a 30 foot minimum, the first 4 hours of moorage are at no charge. Boaters may take any unoccupied slip not marked "reserved" and check-in at the Guest Moorage Office to make payment and obtain a door access code for the restrooms and laundry. If arriving after hours, use the self-registration payment envelope at the Guest Moorage Office window located at the head of 'E' Dock. Office hours are 8am to 8pm daily during the summer months, and 8am to 4pm on the off season. Visitors and locals alike enjoy strolling along the 600 foot boardwalk at Liberty Bay Waterfront Park located next to the Marina.

Coffee shops, restaurants, and gift shops are within easy walking distance of the Marina and many of the buildings reflect a Scandinavian design and motif. Be sure to stop by the Marina Market on Front Street, which carries Scandinavian, German, and other imported groceries. For unique nautical gifts and treasures, visit the Cargo Hold (360-697-1424) also on Front Street.

Poulsbo was settled in the 1880's by Norwegian loggers, farmers, and fishermen, who likened Liberty Bay and the landscape to their homeland. Poulsbo once had one of the largest codfish processing plants for salting and preserving fish as well as processing lutefisk. Locals and visitors can still eat lutefisk at the First Lutheran Church (360-779-2622) at their annual Lutefisk Dinner held on the third Saturday in October. The church is located on a bluff at 18920 Fourth Ave. NE overlooking Poulsbo.

The annual Viking Fest takes place on the weekend around May 17th each year. Celebrations include food, entertainment, folk dancing, and carnival rides, capped off with a fireworks display over Liberty Bay on Friday night. Don't miss the fun Viking Fest Parade held on Saturday with its fearless Viking Warriors and the annual lutefisk eating contest on Sunday. For dates and schedules, go to www.VikingFest.org or call the Poulsbo Visitor Center at (360-779-4848).

The Poulsbo Marine Science Center (360-598-4460) located at the east end of the Marina is worth a visit. Children love the inter-tidal touch tank and the Pacific Octopus, which lives in a 2,000 gallon tank under a dock. The Center's main focus is to educate children in marine science through various educational programs. The Marine Science Center is open to the public from 11am to 4pm, Thursday through Sunday, winter hours may vary.

Poulsbo Guest Marina	360-779-3505	VHF 66A
Portofpoulsbo.com	360-779-9905	

Port of Poulsbo marina with short term and overnight transient space in unoccupied slips. Limited number of reservations taken. Restrooms, showers, laundry, pumpout, and Fuel Dock. Power and water at slips. Dinghy space.

Short-Term: First 4 hours without charge; slips at F Dock with 10 reservations accepted after which first come first serve.

Overnight: Overnight stays in unoccupied slips at .85 per foot with a 30ft minimum. Pay at Guest Moorage Office or use self-registration payment envelope. Reservations accepted for yacht clubs on E Dock for 10 or more boats. Anchorage in Bay.

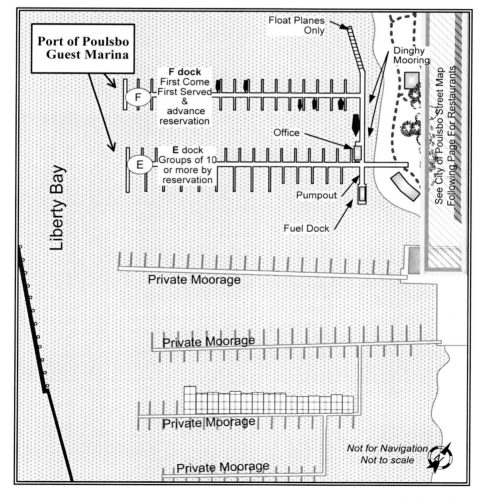

LIBERTY BAY
Port of Poulsbo

POULSBO RESTAURANTS			🍽
Bayside Broiler	Steak, Burgers, Fish	18779 Front St	360-779-9076
Boehms Chocolates	Chocolates, Candy	18864 Front St	360-697-3318
Burrata Bistro	Pasta, Ribs, Seafood	19006 Front 100	360-930-8446
Casa Luna	Mexican Cuisine	18830 Front St	360-779-7676
Checkers	Espresso, Dessert, Ice Cream	18881 Front #E	360-697-2559
Hot Shots Java	Espresso, Pastries, Ice Cream	18881 Front #B	360-779-2171
J.J.'s Fish House	Seafood, Pasta, Salad	18881 Front St	360-779-6609
Liberty Bay Bakery	Pies, Cakes, Pastries	18996 Front St	360-779-2828
Marina Market	European Foods	18882 Front St	360-779-8430
Mor Mor Bistro	Sandwiches, Pizza, Seafood, Meats	18820 Front St	360-697-3449
Poulsbo Woodfired Pizza	Pizza, Calzones	18937E Front St	360-598-4016 (deliveries)
Poulsbohemian	Coffee, Soup, Sandwiches	19003 Front St	360-779-9199
Sheila's Bay Café	Breakfast, Burgers, Sandwiches, Fish	18779 Front St	360-779-2997
Sluys Poulsbo Bakery	Pies, Cakes, Pastries	18924 Front St	360-779-2798
Sogno di Vino	Wine and Spirits	18830 Front St	360-697-8466
That's-A-Some Italian	Pasta, Pizza, Sandwiches	18881 Front St	360-779-2266
The Village Baker	Sandwiches, Desserts	18801 Front 105	360-598-Bake
Tizley's Europa	Deli Sandwiches, Cheese, Wine	18928 Front St	360-394-0082
Voodiez Bar & Grill	Breakfast, Steak, Sandwiches, Burgers	18932 Front St	360-779-6636
Whiskey Creek Ranch House	Burgers, Steaks, Seafood	18801 Front St	360-697-9800

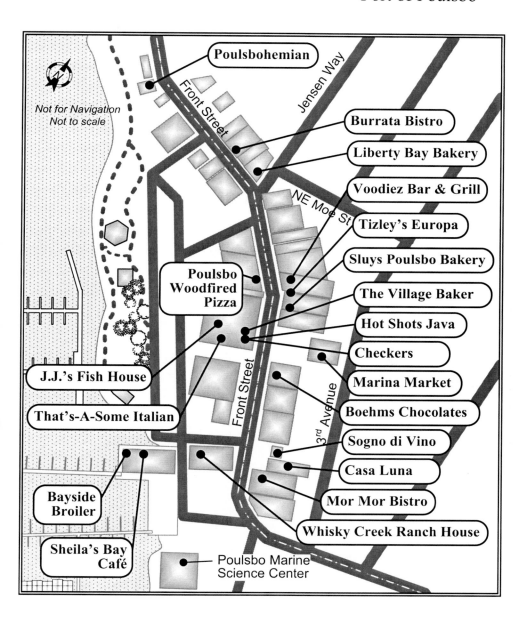

Not for Navigation
Not to scale

Poulsbohemian

Front Street

Jensen Way

Burrata Bistro

Liberty Bay Bakery

NE Moe St

Voodiez Bar & Grill

Tizley's Europa

Sluys Poulsbo Bakery

Poulsbo Woodfired Pizza

The Village Baker

Hot Shots Java

Checkers

J.J.'s Fish House

Front Street

3rd Avenue

Marina Market

Boehms Chocolates

That's-A-Some Italian

Sogno di Vino

Casa Luna

Bayside Broiler

Mor Mor Bistro

Whisky Creek Ranch House

Sheila's Bay Café

Poulsbo Marine
Science Center

LIBERTY BAY
Port of Poulsbo

J.J.'S FISH HOUSE

J.J.'s Fish House is a sharp, modern café just off the Liberty Bay Waterfront Park with a large outdoor patio for summer dining. Specialty seafood dishes along with pasta, burgers, and sandwiches are favorites at J.J.'s. Try the meaty Poulsbo Clam Chowder or the leafy Citrus Salad with grilled chicken, or perhaps a selection of starters like the Grilled Crab Cakes, Steamers, or the Lox Pan Bread with smoked salmon, red onions, capers, and fresh basil. Dinner entrees include the Smoked Salmon Linguine, Grilled Halibut, and Salmon. The Cioppino, a bowl full of clams, mussels, halibut, and cod in a rich, tangy tomato wine broth with herbs and spices is also a good choice. Don't forget to ask about the day's dessert selections.

Lunch	11am – 4pm Daily
Dinner	4pm – 9pm Sun-Thur 4pm – 10pm Fri & Sat Close 1hr earlier winters
Price	Moderate
Outdoor Seating	Yes, Patio Summer Months
Contact	360-779-6609

MOR MOR BISTRO & BAR

The Mor Mor has a pleasing European bistro flare with French and Italian influences in both the menu and décor. The covered brick patio is set with lovely wrought iron furnishings along with beautiful potted flowers and hanging flower baskets. Sheer drapes adorn the windows on the interior with bar-style tables in front and intimate tables near the back. The Mor Mor features locally farmed produce, wild seafood, and natural raised poultry, game, and Oregon raised beef.

Lunch	11am – 5pm Daily
Dinner	5pm – 9pm Daily
Price	Moderate - Expensive
Outdoor Seating	Yes, Patio, Summer Months
Contact	360-697-3449

The dinner menu changes daily and may include the Grilled Oregon Beef Medallions served on goat cheese potato gratin with roasted vegetables and red wind demi-glace or perhaps the Cedar planked Wild Alaskan Salmon served on whipped roasted root vegetables, sautéed sugar snaps, and tarragon nage'. You may want to start with an appetizer like the lightly Fried Calamari Rings, the Meat & Cheese Plate, or the house Marinated Olives. For lunch, try the braised Beef Brisket Sandwich with the Mixed Field Greens Salad or perhaps the Pizza Sicilian. Don't forget to ask about the fine beer, specialty cocktails, and fine wines.

MANCHESTER
Manchester Dock

The village of Manchester offers spectacular views of the Seattle skyline and is just beginning to be discovered by new homeowners and developers. Located on the Olympic Peninsula, west of Blake Island, Manchester offers a 200 foot dock for visiting boaters on a first come, first serve basis at no charge. Stays are permitted during the day, no overnight stays. The North Dock is for boat launch purposes only; use the South Dock for guest moorage. There are pilings spaced about every 20 feet on the south side of the guest dock, providing space suitable for small craft, while the north side of the guest dock is best suited for larger vessels.

A public beach with park-side picnic tables is located upland from the docks. The adorable country-style "Family Inn" restaurant is within easy walking distance and just up Main Street to the corner of Colchester Drive. The Manchester Food Center (360-871-1271) is just upland from the dock and carries groceries, coffee, and pastries. Owners of the Food Center plan to add a café in this new complex in the near future.

Manchester was established in the 1860's and was originally known as Brooklyn after New York's Brooklyn. The name was changed to Manchester in 1892 in honor of Manchester, England. It is interesting to note that property in "Manchester Heights" sold for $25 a lot in 1908. A permanent dock was built that same year and regular steamboat service connected Manchester to Seattle and other communities. In 1940, the U.S. Navy built a pier nearby for refueling ships, which is still used today. Be sure to give this pier a wide berth when passing.

Manchester Dock	253-853-7449 Port
	360-871-0500 Water District

Port of Manchester public dock with adjacent boat launch. South Dock may be used for day use guest moorage, approximately 200 feet with pilings on one side. Restrooms, no power or water at dock. North Dock is used for boat launch purposes and goes dry at low tide.

Short-Term: South Dock for day use at no charge; first come, first serve.

Overnight: No overnight stays.

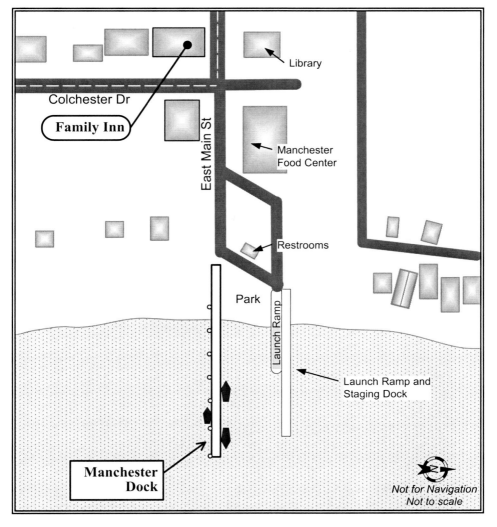

MANCHESTER
Manchester Dock

FAMILY INN 🍽

The Family Inn is a fun country-style restaurant with wood paneling, green wainscoting, antiques, and country western décor. A miniature stage-coach hangs above the food counter and the pub section has a cozy rock fireplace. The dining room is very inviting with white linen tablecloths, flowers, and western photos and art work along with a number of gift items for sale. A covered front porch is popular during the warm months, providing water views and people watching opportunities. The Family Inn is open for breakfast Saturdays and Sundays and daily for lunch and dinner.

Breakfast	8am – 1pm Sat & Sun
Lunch/ Dinner	11am – 8pm Daily
Price	Moderate
Outdoor Seating	Yes, Covered Porch
Contact	360-871-8199

Breakfast includes all the classic favorites like omelets, pancakes, French toast, waffles, steak, and sausage. For lunch try one of the homemade sandwiches or soups, or perhaps the old-fashioned liver & onions. A nice selection of burgers and fish baskets is offered as well, including the Prawns & Chips and the Howie Burger. Pizza and pasta favorites include the Chicken Delight Pizza and the Spaghetti Pomodoro. Evening "comfort foods" include Pot Roast, Chicken Cordon Bleu, Rib-eye Steak, and Meatloaf to name a few. There is something for everyone at the Inn.

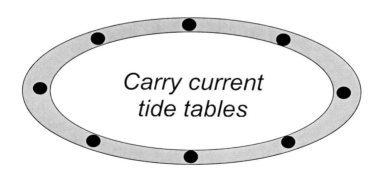

Carry current
tide tables

PORT MADISON
Indianola Dock

The tiny village of Indianola is located on the north bank of Port Madison, northeast of Suquamish and Agate Passage. The Indianola Pier extends several hundred feet from shore and offers a 25 foot access float for visiting boaters. The float is exposed to wind and waves so appropriate fenders and spring lines should be used, the float is available June through mid-September. The views from the pier are captivating and the village has an enchanting appeal, which makes this landing a special stop for lunch. The village consists of a post office, the Bud Merrill Pavilion, the Indianola Community Hall, and the historic Indianola Country Store, which serves freshly made deli sandwiches.

Development of Indianola began with the 1916 formation of the Indianola Beach Land Company to promote real estate sales. A dock and store were built to attract buyers to this vacation community. Most transportation on Puget Sound in the early 20th Century was by steamer; and by 1918 a steamer docked here every weekend, daily ferry service was provided a year later. In 1938 the dock was widened to allow auto access in conjunction with the completion of a road connecting Indianola and Suquamish. The ferry service was discontinued in the fall of 1951 after the Agate Pass Bridge opened and the Washington State Ferries took over ferry service on Puget Sound.

Today, residents take great pride in celebrating "Indianola Days," usually in July or August based on the tide schedule for extended beach access. Throughout the year residents and visitors can attend the Saturday Morning Market from 9:30am to noon, located in the Bud Merrill Pavilion, which is across the road from the Country Store & Deli.

INDIANOLA COUNTRY STORE & DELI

The 1930's Indianola Country Store & Deli is located upland from the public pier and is a convenient stop for lunch and groceries or coffee and sweets. The café area of the store provides seating with antique furnishings and several historic photos and gift items. Sandwich orders are taken at the deli counter with choice of breads and meats, including turkey, roast beef, ham, pastrami, corned beef, and smoked turkey; or you can purchase sliced meats and cheeses to take back to the boat to make your own sandwich creation.	Hours	7:30am – 8:30pm Sun-Thur 7:30am – 9pm Fri & Sat Hours Vary Off Season
	Price	Moderate
	Outdoor Seating	No
	Contact	360-297-3327

Other treats include cinnamon rolls, bagels, espresso, cookies, and even ice cream cones. It has been reported that Martha Stewart stopped at the Indianola Country Store & Deli for a cup of espresso during her travels through Washington State.

Indianola Pier

360-297-3281 Port Office
360-297-3327 Country Store

Port of Indianola pier with a 25 foot guest float to access the village of Indianola for short term visits. Float available June through mid-September.

Short-Term: Short stays of an hour or less at no charge while visiting the Indianola Country Store and village.

Overnight: No overnight stays.

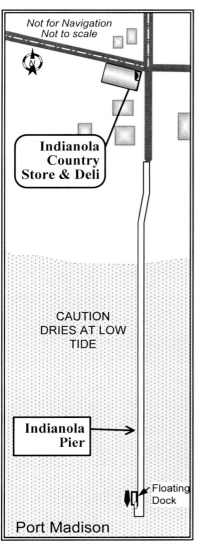

PORT MADISON
Suquamish

The small village of Suquamish is located on the western shore of Port Madison on the Port Madison Indian Reservation, home to the Suquamish tribe. A 435-foot pier was completed in early 2009 along with a 100-foot guest dock for hourly stays. Three buoys located on the south side of the pier provide additional guest moorage.

The Suquamish community has stunning views of Puget Sound, the Seattle skyline, and the Cascade Mountains. The village offers two restaurants, a bar & grill, and a gift shop located upland from the guest dock and a newly constructed 8.5 million dollar Longhouse. The Longhouse serves as a cultural center for special events and classes.

Visitors are welcome to view the Longhouse and the nearby grave site of Chief Sealth (Chief Seattle) located behind St. Peter's Church in the Suquamish Memorial Cemetery. Follow Suquamish Way to NE South Street; the church and cemetery is just a short distance up the hill on South Street. The sacred grave site has two large painted canoes above the headstone in honor of Chief Seattle, who signed the Treaty of Point Elliott in 1855 and delivered the famous speech used to support the cultural and spiritual values of all indigenous people.

A grave-side ceremony is held each year during Chief Seattle Days (360-598-3311) on the third weekend in August. This historic celebration includes Native dance performances, a salmon bake, and canoe races. Tribes from all over Puget Sound come with their canoes to attend the celebration, attracting thousands of spectators. A special Argosy Cruise to Suquamish is being considered as a future offering.

Plans are currently under way to develop a new site for the Suquamish Museum, which is currently located on Sandy Hook Road southwest of Suquamish. Construction on the new museum building, to be located in Suquamish west of the Memorial Cemetery, is slated to begin in 2010.

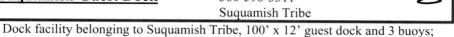

Suquamish Guest Dock	360-598-3311
	Suquamish Tribe

Dock facility belonging to Suquamish Tribe, 100' x 12' guest dock and 3 buoys; first-come, first-serve. No power or water. Quiet zone – no generators.

Short-Term: Hourly stays at no charge; open till 10pm weekdays and until 11pm on weekends.

Overnight: No overnight stays.

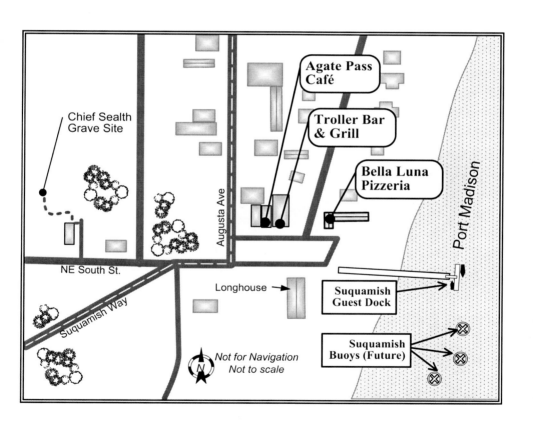

PORT MADISON
Suquamish

AGATE PASS CAFÉ 🍽

This classy café is a recent addition to Suquamish and is fitting for the area's new image and redevelopment. Tables in this cozy café are set with linens topped with brown butcher paper, and the walls are adorned with sculpted art work and lovely wall sconces. The Café serves local wines, beer on tap, and bistro-style meals that change seasonally. Starters include stuffed dates, French onion soup, and manila clams; or begin your meal with the Apple-bleu Salad with spinach, Gala apple, bleu cheese, and candied walnuts.

Dinner	5pm – 9pm Wed-Thur 5pm – 10pm Fri & Sat 3:30pm – 8pm Sundays
Brunch	9am – 2:30pm Sundays
Price	Moderate - Expensive
Outdoor Seating	Yes, Porch, Summer Months
Contact	360-930-0911

For a main, try the pan-seared Sea Scallops with squash mash, or the Game Hen pan-roasted and served with creamy polenta and braised greens. For the finishing touch, enjoy a Meyer Lemon Tart made with a shortbread crust and candied peel.

BELLA LUNA PIZZERIA 🍽️

This casual pizzeria is just upland from the Suquamish guest dock on the edge of a high bank overlooking Port Madison and Agate Pass. This neighborhood eatery serves homemade soups, lasagna, calzones, and specialty pizzas like the Big Dipper BBQ Chicken with sweet & tangy barbeque sauce; or try the Galactic Greek with roasted eggplant, roasted bell peppers, Greek olives, tomatoes, and feta cheese. Burgers and sandwiches are also offered, including the Caramelized Onion & Swiss Burger, the Meatball Sandwich, and the Roasted Veggie.

Breakfast	7am – 11am Mon-Fri 7am – Noon Sat & Sun
Lunch/ Dinner	11am – 9pm Mon-Thur 11am – 10pm Fri & Sat 11am – 8pm Sundays
Price	Moderate
Outdoor Seating	Yes, Deck and Patio, Summer Months
Contact	360-598-5398

A variety of omelets are served at breakfast along with pancakes and sausage available each morning. Eggs Benedict is added to the breakfast menu on Sundays. The views from the summer deck and side patio provide outstanding views and the perfect venue any time of day.

SINCLAIR INLET
Sinclair Inlet Area

Sinclair Inlet sits at the southern extremity of Port Orchard Bay accessed from the east through Rich Passage. The communities of Annapolis and Port Orchard hug the shores of Sinclair Inlet on the south bank. The city of Bremerton lies on the north shore of Sinclair Inlet and is divided by the Port Washington Narrows, which leads into Dyes Inlet. Manette on the northeast side of the Washington Narrows is referred to as North Bremerton and is home to the popular Boat Shed restaurant located next to the Manette Bridge.

The city of Bremerton recently completed an expansion of the Bremerton Marina with the addition of new concrete docks offering ample guest space for visiting boaters. New developments along Bremerton's waterfront include a Convention Center, Boardwalk & Fountains, and the Harborside Fountain Park along with new restaurants, hotels, and condominiums. The City's museums are easily accessible from the docks, including the popular Navy Warship Tours (360-792-2457). Sinclair Inlet is also home to the Puget Sound Naval Shipyard responsible for overhauling, maintaining, and decommissioning of ships.

Located on the south bank of Sinclair Inlet is the Port Orchard Marina offering boaters hourly and overnight guest space and is within easy walking distance of local restaurants and shops. Guests can also visit the restaurants and shops in Bremerton via the Kitsap Transit Foot Ferry (360-373-2877), which makes frequent runs between the two marinas. Additional hourly moorage can be found at the Port Orchard Public Pier (Dekalb Street Pier) located southwest of Port Orchard Marina. Boaters should note that these floats bottom out at low tide as posted. The Public Pier is behind and adjacent to Sinclair Inlet Marina.

Port Orchard was once called Sidney after its pioneer Sidney Stevens from Dekalb, Illinois, who purchased land here in the late 1800's with the intent of creating a town. Bremerton was platted by German immigrant, William Bremer, in 1891. Three years earlier, the U.S. Navy determined that Point Turner between Sinclair Inlet and Dyes Inlet would be an ideal site to establish a shipyard. Bremer and his business partner, Henry Hensel, purchased land near Point Turner and then sold 190 acres to the Navy, which became part of the initial footprint of the Puget Sound Navy Yard.

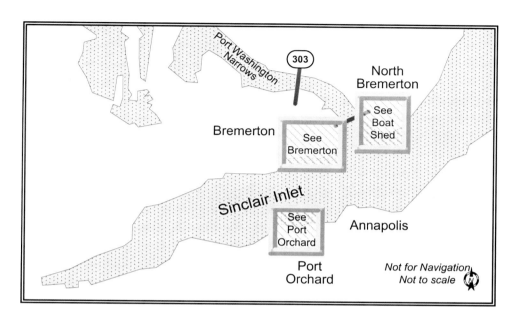

Port Washington Narrows

303

North Bremerton

See Boat Shed

Bremerton

See Bremerton

Sinclair Inlet

See Port Orchard

Annapolis

Port Orchard

Not for Navigation
Not to scale

SINCLAIR INLET
Boat Shed Guest Dock

The Manette Bridge, which spans the Port Washington Narrows in Sinclair Inlet, connects the community of Manette to Bremerton. At the northeast end of the bridge on the Manette waterfront is the popular Boat Shed restaurant with its 40 foot guest float. Docking can be a challenge here due to the current and wind conditions, be sure to have lines and fenders ready and approach against the current. After securing your craft with additional spring lines, you're ready to enjoy this unique nautical venue within steps of the float. The Boat Shed is set on piers over the water and has great views of Sinclair Inlet, the Port Washington Narrows, and the Manette Bridge.

Prior to 1930, the Mosquito Fleet ferry "Pioneer" serviced the crossing to Manette. A toll bridge was constructed by the East Bremerton Improvement Club and opened in June of 1930. Locals had gone door to door selling stock and raised approximately $200,000 for construction of the bridge. Among those present at the opening ceremonies was Jane Garrison, the 106 year old grand-daughter of Chief Seattle. In 1949, the wooden bridge was replaced with the present concrete and steel version. Plans are currently underway to once again update the bridge with construction expected to start in the spring of 2010.

Boat Shed Guest Dock	360-377-2600

Private 40 foot guest float for use by patrons of the Boat Shed restaurant. Be prepared with fenders and lines due to wind and current.

Short-Term: Short term stays while dining at the restaurant.

Overnight: No overnight stays.

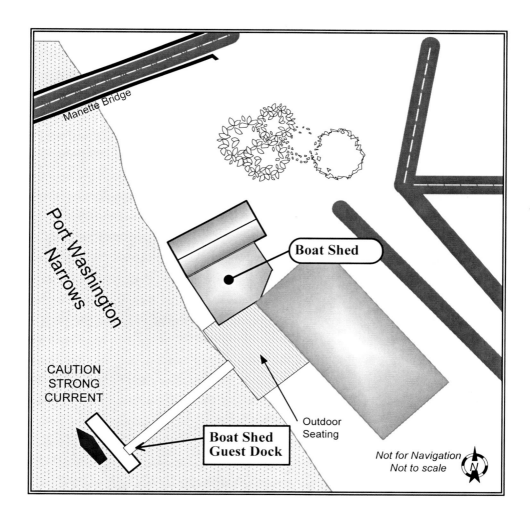

BOAT SHED ◉

The Boat Shed is one of the most unique nautical dining venues on Puget Sound. The restaurant is set on piers over the water with great views from every seat and from the large deck overlooking Sinclair Inlet and the Manette Bridge. Numerous potted flowers are hung from the deck and you may even see a seal swim by from time to time. The Boat Shed has a casual, classy appeal with nice furnishings, fixtures, and bamboo window shades. Black and white photos and oil paintings adorn the walls in the dining room and the separate bar is a favorite with the younger folks.

Lunch/ Dinner	11am – 9pm Sun-Thur 11am – 10pm Fri & Sat
Price	Moderate
Outdoor Seating	Yes, Deck, Summer Months
Contact	360-377-2600

The menu is upscale including fresh seafood, certified Angus beef, burgers & sandwiches, and salads. Try the Raspberry Chicken Salad for lunch or the Sloop Sandwich with corned beef, pastrami, Swiss cheese, sauerkraut, and secret sauce, served on hot rye bread. Entree favorites include the Angus Bleu Cheese New York topped with melted Bleu cheese butter and served with onion straws; or try the Fresh Pacific King Salmon, grilled or blackened. Desserts are made in-house and include the Bailey's Chocolate Cheesecake and the Blackberry Cobbler.

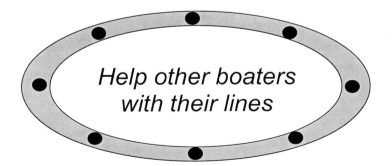

*Help other boaters
with their lines*

SINCLAIR INLET
Port of Bremerton Marina

Bremerton has emerged from a once tired cityscape into a new and exciting waterfront destination, including an expansive new Marina and Boardwalk, a new Conference Center, classy condominiums, hotels, and eateries, along with a beautiful waterfront park. Anthony's Restaurant is located within steps of the Marina and additional eateries are located in the Conference Center Plaza and across the street. An impressive set of stairs with a cascading water feature leads up to the Conference complex from the waterfront Boardwalk.

The Port of Bremerton Marina offers guest slips located on Dock A; the west half of Dock B; and the "Public Dock," which is between docks C & D for a total of 160 slips. Side-tie of 150 feet is available on the "Public Dock" and an additional 650 feet of side-tie on the south end (inside) of the Breakwater. The first 4 hours of moorage are without charge, after which fees are $12/night or .60 per foot over 20ft. on the South Breakwater and $26/night or .65 per foot over 40ft. for a slip at A & B Docks and at the Public Dock. Boaters may take any available space on these docks and on the Breakwater that is not marked "reserved" and should check in at the Marina Office located upland on the Boardwalk to make payment. Office hours are 8:30am to 7:30pm daily June-Sept. and closes at 4:30pm during the off season. Reservations are accepted with a five dollar reservation fee except during major holiday weekends. Be sure to note the gate code on the access gate for re-entry.

Bremerton is known for its excellent museums, including the Naval Memorial Museum (360-479-7447) open daily located just south of the Marina and ferry terminal. Don't miss the fun and attractive Harborside Fountain Park located behind the Naval Museum. The copper clad fountains erupt with bursts of water operated by air driven jets and look like ships going out to sea. The park is a great place for kids of all ages to dip their toes in the fountains and enjoy a picnic lunch overlooking the harbor. Another "must do" is the Navy Warship Tours (360-792-2457) aboard the destroyer, USS Turner Joy. The tour ticket office is located on the north end of the Boardwalk just upland from the Turner Joy vessel. Other points of interest include the Kitsap County Historical Society Museum (360-479-6226) at 280 Fourth Street and the Aurora Valentinetti Puppet Museum (360-373-2992) located at 257 Fourth Street.

Popular summer events include "Concerts on the Boardwalk" held on consecutive Fridays from mid-July through mid-August and include jazz, Latin, light rock, country, and blues bands. The Annual Blackberry Festival is held on Saturday of Labor Day weekend and is the largest festival in Puget Sound with numerous activities, races, and contests as well as the classic Fly-In at the Bremerton Airport. A free Kitsap shuttle bus is available to and from the airport and waterfront activities during the festival. Vendors are open on the Boardwalk offering blackberry treats and blackberry wine along with arts, crafts, entertainers, and live bands. Be sure to arrive early if you want to take in this popular festival.

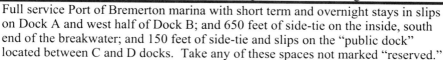

Port of Bremerton Marina   360-373-1035   VHF 66A
www.portofbremerton.org

Full service Port of Bremerton marina with short term and overnight stays in slips on Dock A and west half of Dock B; and 650 feet of side-tie on the inside, south end of the breakwater; and 150 feet of side-tie and slips on the "public dock" located between C and D docks. Take any of these spaces not marked "reserved."

Short-Term: 4 hours of moorage without charge; first come, first serve.

Overnight: Overnight stays at .60/ft on south breakwater and .65/foot in slips. Reservations accepted with $5 fee or first come, first serve.

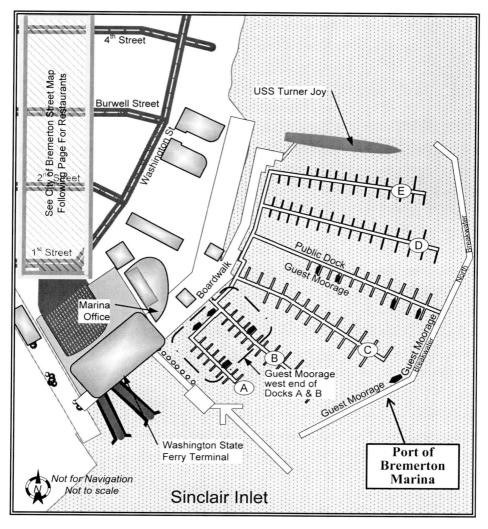

SINCLAIR INLET
Port of Bremerton Marina

BREMERTON RESTAURANTS			🍽
Anthony's	Seafood	20 Washington Ave	360-377-5004
Boston's Pizza	Pizza, Subs, Calzone	206 Burwell Street	360-377-3595 (deliveries)
Cold Stone Creamery	Ice Cream Yogurt	50 Washington Ave	360-782-0276
Fraiche Cup	Espresso, Salads, Sandwiches	105 Washington Av	360-377-1180
Fritz Fry House	Baskets, Sausage, Belgian Beer	100 Washington Av	360-479-1088
Lumpia Teriyaki	Teriyaki	109 Washington Av	360-479-5609
New Delhi	Cuisine of India	221 Washington Av	360-782-2867
South Pacific Sports Bar	Sandwiches, Wraps, Burgers	218 First Street	360-479-1657
Starbucks	Espresso, Pastries	80 Washington Ave	360-373-8105
Subway	Sub Sandwiches	70 Washington Ave	360-377-9140
Taco Del Mar	Mexican Cuisine	90 Washington Ave	360-782-2505
Taco Loco Baja	Mexican Cuisine	200 First Street	360-479-9083 (deliveries)

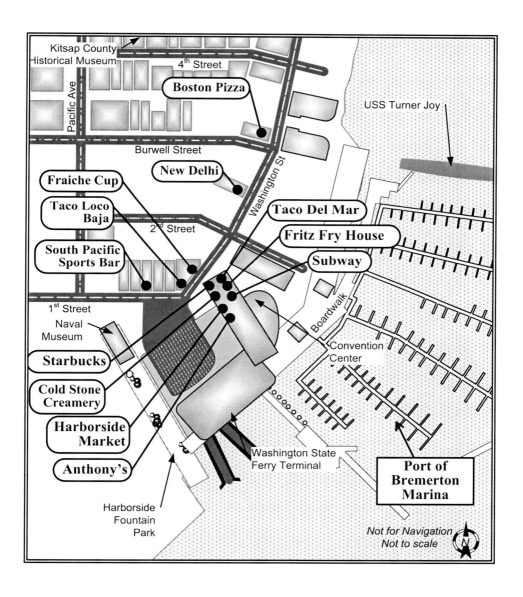

SINCLAIR INLET
Port of Bremerton Marina

ANTHONY'S RESTAURANT

Anthony's Restaurant is located next to the Kitsap Conference Center and has commanding views overlooking Sinclair Inlet, the Bremerton Marina, and the lovely waterfront Boardwalk. During the summer months, you can relax on the attractive outdoor patio while enjoying a seafood appetizer like the Hawaiian Ahi Nachos or the Steamed Sweet Manila Clams. Anthony's restaurants are always beautifully appointed and serve fresh quality seafood, including Alder Planked Salmon, Oven Roasted Halibut, and Fresh Yellowfin Ahi.

Lunch	11am – 4pm Mon-Sat
Dinner	4pm – 9:30pm Sun-Thur 4pm – 10:30pm Fri & Sat
Price	Moderate - Expensive
Outdoor Seating	Yes, Patio, Summer Months
Contact	360-377-5004

You will find quality steaks on the menu as well, like the New York and the Filet Mignon. Come early to enjoy the four-course "sunset dinner" with a choice of appetizer, chowder or salad, an entrée, and dessert, offered Monday through Friday until 6pm. Anthony's at Bremerton has proven to be another quality waterfront venue for this well known Pacific Northwest restaurant.

SINCLAIR INLET
Port of Bremerton Marina

BOSTON'S PIZZA DELI	🍽️

Boston's Pizza Deli is located at the corner of Pacific Ave. and Burwell Street north of the Conference Center. This eatery, located in an attractive red-brick building, offers a wide selection of pizzas and calzones, which are made from fresh dough and homemade sauce. Hot and cold sandwiches are available from the deli like the BBQ Pork and the Meatball Sub along with import, micro, and domestic beer. Dinner specials include Lasagna, Ravioli, Cacciatore dishes, and Linguini with shrimp scampi. Sidewalk seating is available during the summer months in addition to the cozy indoor tables, or you can have your order delivered dockside.

Lunch/ Dinner	11am – 8pm Sun-Thur 11am – 9pm Fri & Sat Hrs Extended Summers
Price	Moderate
Outdoor Seating	Yes, Sidewalk, Summer Months
Contact	360-377-3595

FRAICHE CUP 🍽

Fraiche Cup, located at 105 Washington Ave., is a fun gift shop as well as an espresso shop and lunch-venue. The Fraiche serves excellent espresso, deli sandwiches, and soups along with Swartz Brothers cakes and pastries. You can sit at the bar or at one of the antique tables among the kitchenware, books, and art work while you enjoy a Grilled Foccacia with cheese, pesto, and spinach with a small salad, or perhaps a cup of soup. You will love this fun and friendly shop, open daily, located across the street from the Conference Center.

Lunch/ Dinner	4:30am – 7pm Mon-Fri 6am – 6pm Saturdays 7am – 5:30pm Sundays
Price	Moderate
Outdoor Seating	Yes, Sidewalk, Summer Months
Contact	360-377-1180

SINCLAIR INLET
Port Orchard Marina & Pier

Port Orchard is located southeast of Bremerton on Sinclair Inlet, the Port Orchard Marina is managed by the Port of Bremerton and offers 46 guest slips and 1500 feet of space on each side of the breakwater dock. Enter the Marina from the west side to access the guest slips. The first 4 hours of stay are without charge. Reservations are accepted for stays over four hours with a $5 fee except for major holiday weekends. Fees are based on moorage location and length of vessel and should be paid at the Marina Office upon arrival at which time you will receive a gate access code. Marina Office hours are 8:30am to 6:30pm daily during the summer months, hours vary in the off season. The Marina is conveniently located next to downtown Port Orchard where you will find antique shops, restaurants, and several pubs, including Moon Dogs (360-895-2300) with a fun outdoor beer garden.

Additional short-term moorage is available on the 300 foot Port Orchard Public Pier, which is located southwest of the Port Orchard Marina between Gino's Restaurant and the Sinclair Inlet Marina. Boaters should be aware that these floats "bottom-out" at low tide as posted. The Public Pier sometimes referred to as the Dekalb Street Pier is a nice option for boaters dining at Gino's Restaurant. East of the Pier within easy walking distance is a small park with picnic tables overlooking the boat launch and Sinclair Inlet. A little further east at 577 Bay Street is the cute Bucksnort Coffee stand (360-876-7392), where you can purchase lemonade, smoothies, and tea as well as espresso drinks.

Don't miss the Port Orchard Farmers' Market, one of the oldest and largest in western Washington held in the parking lot next to the Port Orchard Marina on Saturdays May through mid-October. Other events at this location include "Concerts by the Bay" held on Thursday evenings mid-July through mid-August and the classic car show, "The Cruz," held on the 2nd Sunday of August. If you wish to attend an event in Bremerton, you can take one of the historic passenger ferries (360-373-2877) located on the east end of the Port Orchard Marina. The Carlisle II Historic Ferry has been operating for over 90 years and displays historic photos of the earlier Mosquito Fleet. For local history, visit the Sidney Museum (360-876-3693) at 202 Sidney Avenue and the Cabin Museum located two blocks further south at 416 Sidney Avenue, open on weekends during the summer months.

Port Orchard Public Pier	360-876-4991 City 360-876-1700 Police Mngt.	
Port Orchard Public Pier (Dekalb Pier) offering day use while visiting the area; first come, first serve. Pier floats bottom out at low tide. Launch nearby.		
Short-Term:	Short term stays without charge, no moorage after 11pm	
Overnight:	No overnight stays.	

Port Orchard Marina	360-876-5535 VHF 66A
	www.portofbremerton.org

Marina at Port Orchard managed by Port of Bremerton, short-term and overnight stays, check in upon arrival. Restrooms, showers, laundry, pumpout. Power and water on docks. Fuel dock open daily, summers. Activity-float for groups.

Short-Term: 4 hour stays without charge; first come, first serve

Overnight: Overnight stays $26/night or .65/ft over 40ft. in slips; breakwater & transition dock $12-$13/night or .60 to .65/ft. over 20ft.; reservations accepted with a $5 fee.

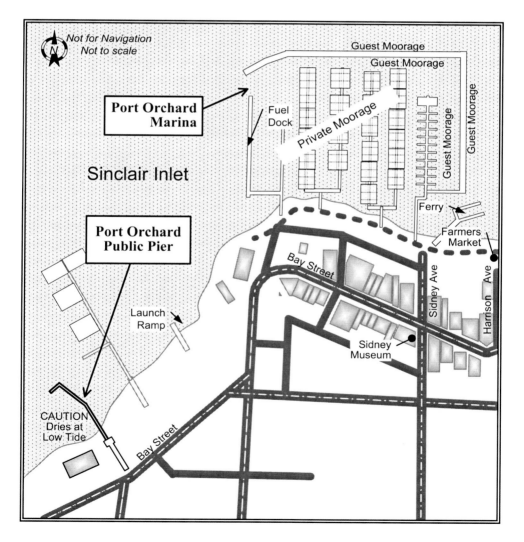

SINCLAIR INLET
Port Orchard Marina & Pier

PORT ORCHARD RESTAURANTS			🍽
Amy's on the Bay	Seafood, Steak, Pasta	100 Harrison Av	360-876-1445
Candy Shoppe	Old-fashioned Candy	833 Bay Street	360-874-2576
Corner Deli	Sandwiches, Soups, Ice Cream	639 Frederick	360-876-8010
Delilah's Cozy Kitchen	Breakfast, Panini, Sandwiches	150 Harrison Av	360-895-6061
Gino's	Seafood, Meats, Sandwiches, Pasta	429 Bay Street	360-874-2075
Hideaway Café	Burgers, Soups, Sandwiches	807 Bay Street (back side)	360-895-4418
Juwapas	Vegetarian, Juice Bar	834 Bay Street	360-876-0501
Los Cabos	Mexican Cuisine	642 Bay Street	360-895-7878
Moon Dogs	Spirits, Pub Grub	714 Bay Street	360-895-2300
Morningside Bakery	Baked Goods, Sweets	707 Bay Street	360-876-1149
Wine Cellar	Wine Shop	120 Harrison Av	360-895-9463

SINCLAIR INLET
Port Orchard Marina & Pier

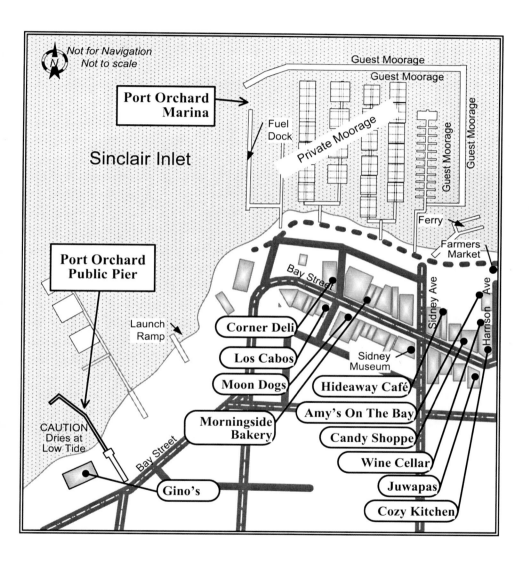

SINCLAIR INLET
Port Orchard Marina & Pier

AMY'S ON THE BAY   ¶○¶

Amy's on the Bay is located east of the Port Orchard Marina next to the Marina Park with beautiful views of Sinclair Inlet and the lights of Bremerton during the evening hours. The dining room has a combination of tables and booths, a cozy fireplace, and garage-style doors that pull open during the summer months extending the space out onto the patio. Amy's is a popular venue and is especially busy when the summer Saturday Market next door is underway. The lunch menu includes burgers, fish tacos, and sandwiches along with soups and salads.

Lunch/ Dinner	11am – 4pm Daily
	4pm – 9pm Sun-Thur
	4pm – 10pm Fri & Sat
	Hours Vary Off Season
Price	Moderate - Expensive
Outdoor Seating	Yes, Patio, Summer Months
Contact	360-876-1445

Dinner entrees include seafood and pasta dishes and natural mid-west Angus steaks like the hand-cut New York, or try the Sirloin Steak & Alaskan King Crab Combo. Duck, lamb, and pork are included under the Seasonal Selections. Entrees are served with choice of roasted red potatoes, garlic mashed potatoes, or jasmine rice with seasonal vegetables. Amy's opened in April of 2006 as a fine dining venue.

GINO'S

Gino's restaurant is conveniently located next to the Port Orchard Public Pier (Dekalb Pier) with wonderful views of Sinclair Inlet and the Olympic Mountains. The restaurant has floor to ceiling windows to take advantage of the views and the lovely patio has a garden-style brick windbreak. The interior is nicely appointed with modern furnishings and fixtures, offering individual tables, a bar, and window-side booths. Restaurateur Gino was born and raised in Peru and brings a personal touch to the varied menu.

Lunch/	11am – 4pm Daily
Dinner	4pm – 9pm Sun-Thur 4pm – 10pm Fri & Sat
Price	Moderate - Expensive
Outdoor Seating	Yes, Patio, Summer Months
Contact	360-874-2075

For lunch Gino offers sandwiches, pizza, and salads like the Meat Balls Sandwich and Nonna's Wild Greens with sun-dried cranberries, candied walnuts, and Gorgonzola crumbles with grilled pears in Balsamic vinaigrette. The dinner menu has a pasta and seafood focus along with beef, chicken, and veal selections. Try the Halibut prepared in a roasted garlic cream sauce served with Yukon Gold mashed potatoes; or try the Twin Beef Tenderloin topped with cheese and figs in a red wine reduction. Desserts include blackberry cobbler, crème brulee, and tiramisu.

Edmonds **175**
 Edmonds Marina 175

Everett **179**
 Port of Everett 179

Holmes Harbor **185**
 Freeland 185

Kingston **189**
 Kingston Marina 189

Langley **195**
 Langley Marina 195

Mukilteo **201**
 Mukilteo Public Dock 201

Port Hadlock **207**
 Irondale Dock 207
 Port Hadlock Marina 211

Port Ludlow **215**
 Port Ludlow Marina 215

Port Townsend **221**
 Port Townsend 221

North Sound

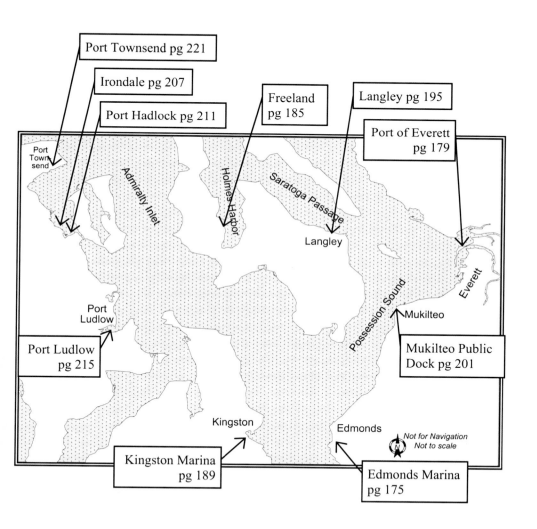

Port Townsend pg 221

Irondale pg 207

Port Hadlock pg 211

Freeland pg 185

Langley pg 195

Port of Everett pg 179

Port Ludlow pg 215

Mukilteo Public Dock pg 201

Kingston Marina pg 189

Edmonds Marina pg 175

Port Townsend

Admiralty Inlet

Holmes Harbor

Saratoga Passage

Langley

Port Ludlow

Possession Sound

Mukilteo

Everett

Kingston

Edmonds

Not for Navigation
Not to scale

EDMONDS
Edmonds Marina

The Port of Edmonds offers boaters grand views of Puget Sound, sandy beaches, and a lovely seaside promenade along with four eateries within easy walking distance of the Port:

EDMONDS PORT RESTAURANTS		
Anthony's Beach Café	Seafood, Burgers, Chicken	425-771-4400
Anthony's Restaurant	Seafood, Steak	425-771-4400
Arnies	Sandwiches, Seafood, Steak	425-771-5688
Waterfront Café	Breakfast, Burgers, Sandwiches, Baskets	425-743-9590 (Charter Office)

Be sure to visit the specialty gift shop "Faces of the NW" (425-771-2000), located next to the Waterfront Café where you can purchase Northwest prints, glass art, jewelry, and fleece wear.

Transient guest space is located on docks 'I' through 'L' on a first come, first serve basis for 4 hours without charge. Portions of these docks may be marked in red for prior reservations from time to time. Stays over four hours and overnight stays are 90 cents per foot per day. Visiting vessels are required to register upon arrival at the Port Office located upland, which is open from 7am to 7pm daily during the summer months and closes at 5pm on the off season. If arriving after hours, use the self-registration payment box at the fuel dock.

Edmonds was founded by George Brackett, who in the late 1800's came ashore after paddling a canoe looking for timber north of Seattle. He purchased land to build his home and town that is now known as Brackett's landing and the City of Edmonds. During the early 1900's, shingle mills stretched all along the Edmonds waterfront. Over time the large trees were cut down and mills began to close, the last mill closed in 1951.

Edmonds Marina	425-774-0549	VHF 16/69	
www.portofedmonds.org	425-775-4588 Harbor Master		

Port of Edmonds marina with hourly and overnight transient moorage with 1,000 feet of side-tie and unoccupied slips. Restrooms, showers, laundry, pumpouts. Power and water on docks. Fuel Dock.

Short-Term: 4 hour stays without charge; first come, first serve.

Overnight: Overnight stays .90/foot per day, check-in at office or use payment box at fuel dock. Reservations accepted.

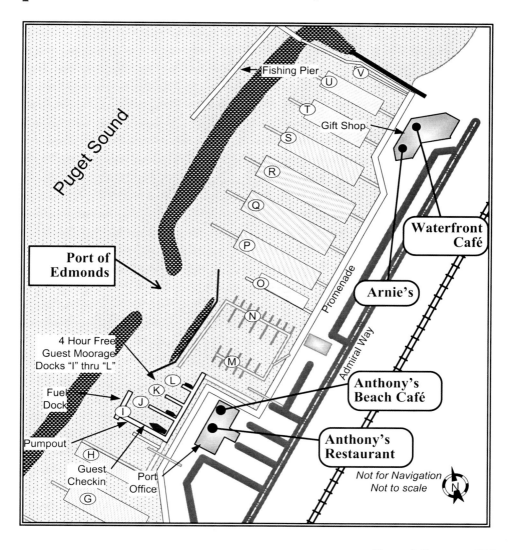

EDMONDS
Edmonds Marina

ANTHONY'S BEACH CAFÉ

This fun café with its beach theme décor has colorful ribbon hanging from the ceilings and cute swimming suits on human wood figures on the bathroom doors. Planter boxes just outside the windows are filled with beautiful flowers of different colors and there is even a sandbox with toys for the children. The Beach Café offers "beach tacos" and "beach bowls & baskets" along with other seafood dishes, burgers, and grilled chicken. The Hawaiian Cobb Salad with fresh mango, bacon, avocado, tomato, and baby shrimp on seasonal greens with basil vinaigrette & crumble blue cheese dressing is a house favorite as is the Barbequed Garlic Prawns with garlic butter, Cajun spices, basil, and red potatoes.

Lunch/ Dinner	11am – 9pm Mon-Thur 11am – 9:30pm Fri & Sat Noon – 9pm Sundays Hours Vary Off Season
Price	Moderate
Outdoor Seating	Yes, Patio, Summer Months
Contact	425-771-4400

ARNIES

Arnies has been an Edmonds icon for many years with spectacular views of the Edmonds waterfront and close-up views of the ferry traffic. The dining room has an open-floor plan with a large comfortable bar and a covered deck for outdoor dining during the summer months. Arnies serves a selection of meat and seafood dishes along with salads, pasta, and sandwiches. Try the seared fish tacos with citrus marinated mahi fillets seared and wrapped in warm flour tortillas with chipotle-lime mayonnaise, cabbage, and fresh salsa; or try the pit roasted smoked salmon with lemon beurre blanc and fried capers. Arnies offers an early bird three-course dinner from 4pm to 6pm, Sunday through Friday.

Lunch	11:30am – 4pm Mon-Sat
Dinner	4pm – 9pm Sun-Thur 4pm – 10pm Fri & Sat
Brunch	10am – 2pm Sundays
Price	Moderate
Outdoor Seating	Yes, Deck, Summer Months
Contact	425-771-5688

EVERETT
Port of Everett

Everett located in Port Gardner northeast of Mukilteo in Possession Sound sits behind Jetty Island along the Snohomish River and offers the second largest marina on the Pacific Coast. Two substantial concrete floats (1800 feet of space) running north and south in front of the Port of Everett Marina basin are available for transient moorage. Unoccupied slips are used for transient space as well when available during the summer months. The boat basin runs east and west with a mile-long esplanade leading to several restaurants, the lovely Port Gardner Inn (425-252-6779), and the Port of Everett Marina Office, which is open daily from 8am to 5pm Mon-Fri and until 4pm Sat and Sun. For ADA wheelchair access, use the guest float at the east end of the south basin docks for drop off and pick up. Guest moorage is based on a first come, first serve basis; however reservations are accepted June through August (Memorial Day – Labor Day). Short-term stays up to 6 hours are without charge. For stays of 6 or more hours, use the self-pay stations located at the head of the docks. Rates vary from .55 per foot to .75 per foot depending on the season.

The 12th Street Yacht Basin, designed for larger yachts, is located just north of the Port of Everett Marina and offers approximately 42 slips for visiting boaters. Fees are payable at the self-pay station at the head of the ramp. The access gate at the guest dock slides open.

Adjacent to the 12th Street Yacht Basin just to the north is a 13-lane launch ramp and the Everett Marine Park with 700 feet of guest moorage, use the pay station at the head of the dock, overnight is permitted but there is no water or power at this dock.

During the summer months of July through August, a foot ferry leaves from the 10th Street Boat Launch, taking visitors across the channel to Jetty Island. Jetty Island is accessible by private boat and is a must for those who enjoy sandy beaches, swimming, and seaside campfires. Leave your pets aboard as this 2 mile-long, half-mile wide, Island is a refuge for many species of birds. Guest space at the dock is on a first come, first serve basis at no charge with an overnight limit of one night per visit. Approximate 300 feet of space is available at the Jetty Island guest dock.

The Port of Everett is full of activity, especially during the summer months. Clubs and groups can reserve the "Activity Barge" (425-388-0664), which has picnic tables, a barbeque, and dockside power. Don't miss the summer concert series including rock, jazz, salsa, and soul music held at the east end of the esplanade between Meyer's Café and Lombardi's Restaurant in the evenings as scheduled. On Sundays be sure to visit the Everett Farmers' Market located on the boardwalk between Lombardi's and the Scuttlebutt Brewing Company. The Market runs from 11am to 4pm May through September.

Points of historic interest at the Port include the Weyerhaeuser Building constructed in 1923 as a lavish office building that showcased the company's wood products. Designed in the Gothic style by Seattle architect Carl Gould, the building looks more like a mansion than an office building. The building was sold to the Port of Everett in 1983 for one dollar and barged from the Weyerhaeuser Mill site and re-sited at its present location near Meyer's Café and the "Inn at Port Gardner." The Weyerhaeuser building was recently purchased by an individual.

Be sure to stop by at the entrance to the 10th Street Boat Launch where you will see a shed protecting the remains of the two-masted schooner Equator, which was built in 1888 in San Francisco. The most famous passenger of this 76-ton sailing vessel was poet and novelist Robert Louis Stevenson, who sailed from Honolulu to the Gilbert Islands aboard the Equator.

EVERETT
Port of Everett

Port of Everett Marina	425-259-6001 VHF 16
	www.portofeverett.com

Port of Everett marina with 1800 feet of side-tie and unoccupied slips for guest moorage. Restrooms, showers, laundry, pumpout. Power and water on docks. Wheelchair access. Fuel Dock.

Short-Term: 6 hours stay without charge; first come, first serve

Overnight: Over 6 hours and overnight stays .55/ft to .75/ft, use payment station at head of docks. Reservations accepted June – Aug.

12 Street Yacht Basin	425-259-6001 VHF 16
	www.portofeverett.com

Port of Everett facility north of the marina for larger yachts with 24 slips for short-term and overnight stays. Restrooms, showers, laundry, travel-lift, pumpout. Power and water at docks.

Short-Term: 6 hours stay without charge; first come, first serve.

Overnight: Overnight stays .55/ft to .75/ft, use payment station at head of ramp. Reservations accepted June - Aug.

Everett Marine Park	425-259-6001 VHF 16
	www.portofeverett.com

Port of Everett marine park with a 12-lane launch ramp and 700 feet of guest moorage. No power or water on docks. No upland facilities.

Short-Term: 6 hours stay without charge; first come, first serve

Overnight: Overnight permitted, use payment station at head of dock. No reservations; first come, first serve.

Jetty Island Dock	425-259-6001 Port
	Everett Parks Department

Everett Parks Dept guest dock on Jetty Island with 300 ft of space for hourly and maximum one night stay. Restrooms, no showers. No power or water at docks. Note currents can be strong.

Short-Term: Day use stays at no charge; first come, first serve.

Overnight: Overnight stay at no charge with a limit of one night per visit; first come, first serve.

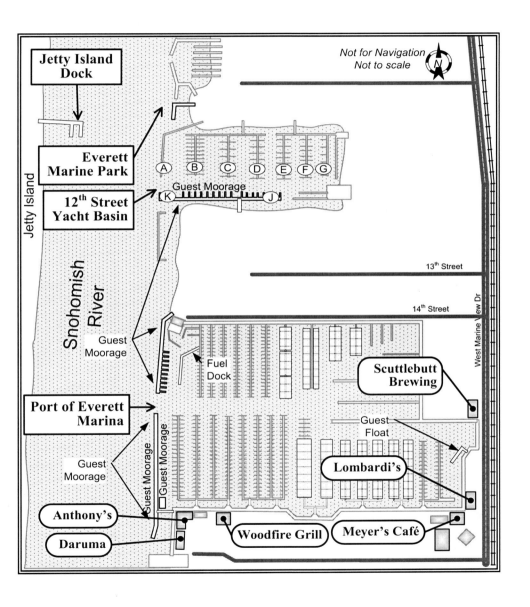

EVERETT
Port of Everett

EVERETT PORT RESTAURANTS			🍽
Anthony's Homeport	Breakfast, Seafood, Steaks	1726 W Marine View	425-252-3333
Anthony's Woodfire Grill	Seafood, Steaks, Rotisserie Meats	1722 W Marine View	425-258-4000
Daruma	Japanese Cuisine	1728 W Marine View	425-339-2307
Lombardi's	Italian Cuisine	1620 W Marine View	425-252-1886
Meyer's Café	Sandwiches, Panini, Salads	1700#C W Marine View Dr.	425-259-3875
Scuttlebutt Brewing	Burgers, Fish, Sandwiches	1524 W Marine View	425-257-9316

LOMBARDI'S 🍽

Lombardi's is a favorite Italian neighborhood venue with two other locations, one in Ballard and another in Issaquah. Lombardi's at Everett is located at the east end of the Port of Everett Marina. The pleasant interior has warm, rich colors with a separate bar featuring cocktails, beer, wine, and non-alcoholic drinks. Window-side seating and the lovely outdoor patio overlooks the Marina, a great place to enjoy a glass of fine wine and watch people stroll along the boardwalk. Lombardi's Italian fare includes panini, pizza, salads, and pasta and seafood dishes. For dinner try the Ravioli and Smoked Salmon or perhaps the Penne Siciliana with pancetta, sweet Italian sausage, tomatoes, peppers, and garlic; or stop by for lunch to enjoy an Italian Grinder with ham, salami, mortadella, Provolone cheese, and olive relish on a ciabatta.

Lunch	11:30am – 3pm Mon-Fri Noon – 3pm Sat & Sun
Dinner	3pm – 9pm Sun-Thur 3pm – 9:30pm Fri & Sat
Happy Hr.	3pm – 6pm Daily and 8pm - Close
Price	Moderate
Outdoor Seating	Yes, Patio, Summer Months
Contact	425-252-1886

ANTHONY'S HOMEPORT

Anthony's Homeport restaurant is located next to the south concrete guest float/dock at the Port of Everett Marina overlooking Possession Sound; look for the red roofed building sporting a lighthouse motif incorporated into the roof design. The outdoor patio with umbrella shaded tables is quite popular during the summer months and the views are equally pleasing from window-side seats in the lovely interior. This Anthony's venue has an excellent Sunday Brunch, including waffles, crepes, omelettes, and Eggs Benedict like the Dungeness Crab Cakes with poached eggs and sautéed spinach with Hollandaise sauce; or try the Blueberry Crepes or New Orleans French Toast with a hint of orange, served with alder smoked bacon and maple syrup.

Lunch	11am – 3pm Mon-Sat
Dinner	4:30pm – 9:30pm Mon-Thur 4:30pm – 10:30pm Fri & Sat 3pm – 9:30pm Sundays
Brunch	10am – 2pm Sundays
Price	Moderate - Expensive
Outdoor Seating	Yes, Patio Deck, Summer Months
Contact	425-252-3333

Lunch favorites include Alder Planked Salmon, Maury Island Quiche, and Willapa Bay Oysters. Dinners include shellfish, steaks, and dishes from the "Tonight's Fish" fresh sheet like the Roasted Garlic Crab from the San Juan Islands and the Alaskan Lingcod. Don't forget to finish off with the Blackberry Cobbler, a signature dessert.

HOLMES HARBOR
Freeland

The private dock for the Holmes Harbor Golf Course and the Beachfire Grill is located northwest of Freeland on the west bank of Holmes Harbor on Whidbey Island. A 160 foot dock with two 40-foot cap ends was installed in the fall of 2007. The north 40 foot end cap is available to visiting boaters while playing at the 18-hole golf course and/or dining at the Beachfire Grill. The remaining portion of the dock is leased out. Visiting boaters with vessels larger than 40 feet may call ahead to check on available space. The guest dock is available to boaters May through September; call the Pro Shop (360-331-2363) with any questions regarding transient moorage. A paved roadway/pathway leads up the hill to the Clubhouse and Beachfire Grill overlooking Holmes Harbor.

South Whidbey Island was first charted by Lieutenant Charles Wilkes of the U.S. Navy in 1841 as "Whidbys Island," Wilkes named the inlet on the east side of the Island after one of his crew members, Doctor Silas Holmes. Early homesteaders included Isaac Ebey and Tom Coupe, whose names remain prominent on the Island today. In 1899, three Seattle visionaries Henry Stevens, George Daniels, and Henry White platted a town made up of five-acre parcels; and in January of 1900, filed the incorporation papers for Freeland.

Holmes Harbor Beach Club

360-331-2363 Pro Shop
206-529-3903 Schuster Group

Private 160 foot dock with a 40-foot end cap on the north for patrons of the Beachfire Grill and/or the Holmes Harbor Golf Course; available May-Sept. Vessels over 40 ft. may call on available space at 160 ft. dock. Boat launch southward at Freeland.

Short-Term: Hourly stays at no charge while playing at the golf course and/or dining at the Beachfire Grill.

Overnight: No overnight stays.

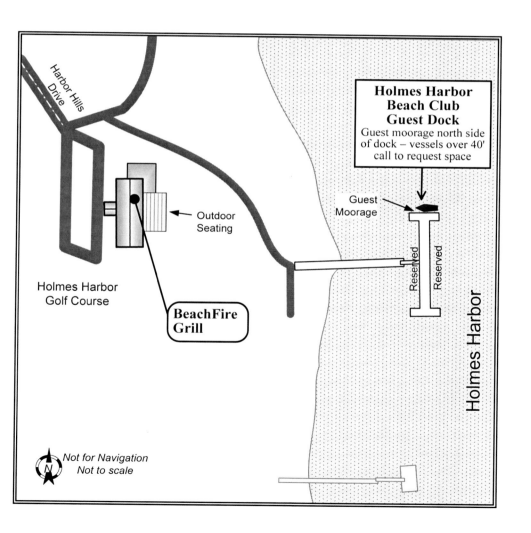

HOLMES HARBOR
Freeland

BEACHFIRE GRILL

The Beachfire Grill located in the Holmes Harbor Clubhouse has outstanding views from the outdoor deck and the expansive dining room, which sports cherry wood furnishings, open wood beam ceilings, and large picture windows. The separate bar is a popular stop for drinks and "small plates" after a game of golf; favorite plates include Crispy Calamari, Penn Cove Mussels, and Crab Cakes served with citrus aioli and cabbage slaw. Locals and visitors alike enjoy the dining room for lunch and dinner, serving sandwiches, burgers, pasta dishes, and

Lunch/Dinner	11:30am – 8:30pm Sun-Thur 11am – 9pm Fri & Sat
Bar	11:30am – 9pm Daily Hrs Vary Off Season
Price	Moderate
Outdoor Seating	Yes, Patio Deck, Summer Months
Contact	360-331-2363

Beachfire classics like the Rib Eye Steak and the Slow Roasted Prime Rib. Pasta dishes include the Roasted Vegetable Ravioli, or try the Crab Fettuccine with sweet rock crab and parmesan in a smoked salmon and caper sauce. Don't forget the Tiramisu or the Beachfire Brule for dessert, or perhaps a special drink like Lemoncello or the Godiva Chocolate Liqueur.

KINGSTON
Kingston Marina

Kingston, known as the "Little City by the Sea," offers a protected marina in Appletree Cove with 49 transient guest slips located just behind the breakwater on a first come, first serve basis; reservations are accepted with a three-day advance notice. Check in at the Marina Office located upland next to the Kingston ferry terminal to make payment and receive an access code for the laundry and marina restrooms. Office hours are 8am to 8pm daily during the summer months and open until 5pm in the off season. Payment may be made after hours at the self-registration payment box below the Marina Office next to the showers. The first two hours of moorage are without charge. Although the Marina is located near the ferry terminal, it is well protected with a high breakwater and has a sense of remoteness and beauty admired by visiting boaters.

The Mike Wallace Park, overlooking the Marina, offers picnic tables and barbecues and has public restrooms. Visiting boaters are also welcome to use the picnic tables located on the guest dock. The Kingston Farmers' Market is held in the Park from 9am to 2:30pm on Saturdays from mid-April to mid-October, where you can purchase fresh produce, local handmade arts and crafts, purchase "eats," and enjoy live music. Public music performances are held in August every Tuesday evening from 6:30pm to 8pm and are co-sponsored by the Port of Kingston. Don't miss the lovely walking trail along the 400 feet of sandy beach owned by the Port. The beach is located on the east side of the ferry vehicle loading area and can be accessed by a set of stairs.

Kingston offers a number of fun restaurants located along its lovely tree-lined main street (Hwy 104). In addition to enjoying the restaurants and coffee shops, be sure to stop by the Kingston Art Gallery (360-297-5133) at NE Kingston Rd. & Hwy 104, which houses quality paintings and art pieces available for purchase.

Kingston's colorful history began in the mid to late 1800's, when Michael King purchased an 1869 cabin in Appletree Cove built by an earlier homesteader, W.S. Ladd and his wife, Caroline. Around 1878, Michael King started a logging camp and built bunkhouses and shacks along the shore for his work crew. When King finished his logging business here in 1882, he left the shacks behind, which became living quarters for drifters, squatters, and old loggers. Residents of a higher standing started moving into the area and began referring to the collection of shacks as "King's Town," which was later shortened to Kingston.

Kingston Marina	360-297-3545 VHF 65A
	www.portofkingston.org

Port of Kingston marina with 49 guest slips up to 50 feet for short term and overnight stays. Restrooms, showers, laundry, pumpout. Power and water at docks. Fuel Dock open 8am to 4:45pm and 7:45pm weekends. Launch nearby.

Short-Term: 2 hours stay without charge; first come, first serve.

Overnight: Stays over 2 hours and overnight stays range from .65 per foot to .75 per foot per day; reservations accepted 3-days in advance. Pay at office or registration payment box below office.

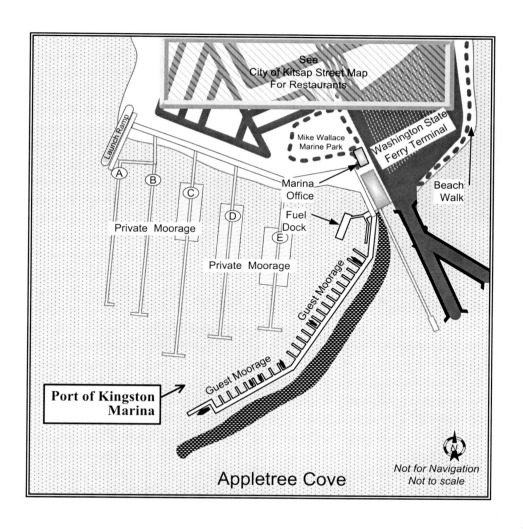

KINGSTON
Kingston Marina

KINGSTON RESTAURANTS			🍽
104 Trolley	Hot Dogs, Popcorn, Ice Cream	Next to Park and Ferry Line	No Phone
Apple Tree Deli	Breakfast, Sandwiches, Soups	11252 Hwy 104	360-297-2102
Coffee Exchange	Espresso, Pastries, Panini, Smoothies	11229 Hwy 104	360-297-7817
Drifters Bar/Lounge	Burgers, Fish, Sandwiches	11265 Hwy 104	360-297-7773
Drifters Espresso Bar	Espresso, Fish, Burgers, Sandwiches	11265 Hwy 104	360-297-4400
Filling Station Pub	Breakfast, Burgers, Sandwiches, Baskets	11200 Hwy 104	360-297-7732
J'aime Les Crepes	Espresso, Crepes, Ice Cream	11264 Hwy 104	360-297-5886
Luna Belle	Italian Cuisine	11227 Hwy 104	360-297-2220
Main Street Ale House	Seafood, Chicken, Steak, Wraps	11225 Hwy 104	360-297-0440
Salsa	Burritos, Tacos	11252 Hwy 104	360-297-3775 (take-out)
Westside Pizza	Pizza Take Out	25955 Ohio Ave	360-297-6800 (deliveries)

KINGSTON
Kingston Marina

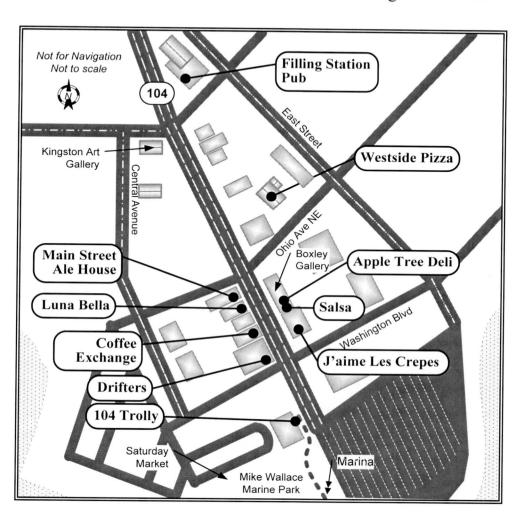

Not for Navigation
Not to scale

104

Filling Station Pub

East Street

Kingston Art Gallery

Central Avenue

Westside Pizza

Ohio Ave NE

Boxley Gallery

Main Street Ale House

Apple Tree Deli

Luna Bella

Salsa

Washington Blvd

Coffee Exchange

J'aime Les Crepes

Drifters

104 Trolly

Saturday Market

Marina

Mike Wallace Marine Park

KINGSTON
Kingston Marina

J'AIME LES CREPES

Hours	5am – 10pm Mon-Fri 7am – 11pm Sat & Sun Close 9pm Off Season
Price	Moderate
Outdoor Seating	Yes, Sidewalk, Summer Months
Contact	360-297-5886

Expect a line of folks at the J'aime Les Crepes eager to place an order for espresso and sweet or savory crepes, especially during the summer months. Two tables are available inside but most of the seating is outdoors on the lovely garden patio and sidewalk. Most people can't resist these sweet crepes like the Belgian Dark Chocolate with caramel, pecans, and whipped cream; or try the Powdered Sugar & Lemon with a scoop of vanilla ice cream. Additional treats include shakes, floats, and malts along with ice cream flavors served in waffle or sugar cones.

Savory crepes like the Smoked Salmon with cream cheese and green onions, or the Grilled Chicken with provolone cheese, spinach, toasted almonds, and lemon herb sauce, make great lunch or light dinner selections. Don't miss this little touch of France in Kingston.

MAIN STREET ALE HOUSE

The nicely appointed Main Street Ale House has an intimate wainscoted dining room with mahogany wood booths upholstered in paisley prints and a separate pub room where folks gather to enjoy karaoke and Jam Night on the weekends. Both the dining room and pub have a warm, rich appeal with a mix of original art and old prints adorning the sage green walls. The food is upscale as well like the Oven Roasted Halibut with lemon beurre blanc; or try the Lemon Cream Prawn Pasta, or perhaps the Alder Planked Wild Salmon with a select wine.

Lunch/ Dinner	11am – 9pm Sun-Thur 11am – 9:30pm Fri & Sat Ale House Open Late Hours Vary Off Season
Price	Moderate
Outdoor Seating	Yes, Deck, Summer Months
Contact	360-297-0440

Slow Roasted Prime Rib is offered every Friday, Saturday, and Sunday evenings. Be sure to ask about other evening specials like the Oyster Platter. For lunch, you can enjoy the nice deck off the dining room overlooking Appletree Cove while you enjoy a Salmon Caesar Wrap with a Pear Salad, and micro brew.

LANGLEY
Langley Marina

Langley is one of the most charming towns in Puget Sound located on beautiful Whidbey Island on a bluff overlooking Saratoga Passage and the Cascade Mountains. The Langley Boat Harbor, located on the east end of town below the bluff, offers transient moorage May through September for hourly and overnight stays on a first come, first serve basis. Guests may take any slip or side-tie not marked "reserved" and make payment at the self-registration payment box at the head of the gangway/pier. A $5 tie-up fee is accessed from 8am to 10pm. Overnight rates are based on length of vessel as posted on the payment envelope and range from $5 per night to $42 per night. The Boat Harbor is creative when it comes to finding space for visitors and may move boats around as needed. The Boatyard Inn (360-221-5120) is located next to the Boat Harbor and is where you will find a road leading up to the town of Langley. The lovely Saratoga Inn (360-221-5801) is located near the top of the road. Make a right turn to walk into the heart of Langley for the many fine eateries, coffee shops, book stores, clothing boutiques, and gift shops.

There are many interesting places to eat and shop so set aside enough time for walking and exploring. Be sure to stop by the Star Store Market (360-221-2468) at 201 First Street, a market and mercantile carrying kitchenware, clothing, gifts, and groceries. For unique nautical gifts and décor, visit Cascadia Nauticals (360-221-3747), and for all your pet supplies visit Myken's (360-221-4787), both shops are located on 1st Street. The five-star "Inn at Langley" (360-221-3033) and "Spa Essencia" (360-221-0991) are located at the west end of 1st Street. "The Chef's Dining Room" at the Inn offers a special menu on Fridays, Saturdays, and Sundays with a 2-3 hour presentation dining experience, call for information and reservations. Just before you reach the Inn you will pass the historic Dog House Tavern built in 1908; the street level served as a mercantile, the upstairs as a game club, and the bottom level as a basketball court for the high school. Stop for sandwiches, burgers, or a drink to experience the old wood floors, antiques, and ambiance of an earlier time. Chocolate lovers will not want to miss One Angle Place located on 2nd Street; and for a fun old-fashioned breakfast venue, visit The Braeburn country kitchen across 2nd Street from the chocolate shop.

History buffs will enjoy the South Whidbey Historical Museum (360-221-2101) located at 312 2nd Street, open 1pm to 4pm on Saturdays and Sundays. Langley is surrounded by beautiful farms and country roads, which can be enjoyed via moped. Moped rentals are available at Whidbey Island Moped (360-221-5152) at 308 1st Street in the Hellebore Glass Studio Building. They can provide maps and suggested routes. Be sure to visit the Whidbey Island Winery (360-221-2040) south on Langley Rd. This family-run winery has gained a reputation for quality wines from grapes grown on the Island and grapes from Eastern Washington vineyards. The Winery has a nice gift shop, picnic tables, and pretty vineyards, hours are noon to 5pm (closed Tue.) during the summer months and closed both Monday and Tuesday in the off season.

Langley Boat Harbor

360-221-4246 #4
360-221-1120 Harbormaster

The Langley Boat Harbor has transient space in 41 slips up to 35ft. and 200 feet of side-tie available May-September; first come, first serve. Restrooms, showers, pumpout. Power and water on docks. Launch ramp (high tide only).

Short-Term: $5 tie-up fee from 8am to 10pm, use pay station at head of pier.

Overnight: Rates for overnight stays vary as posted on envelope ($5-$42 per night); first come first serve. Use pay station at head of pier. Boats may be moved around for other visitors. Anchorage nearby.

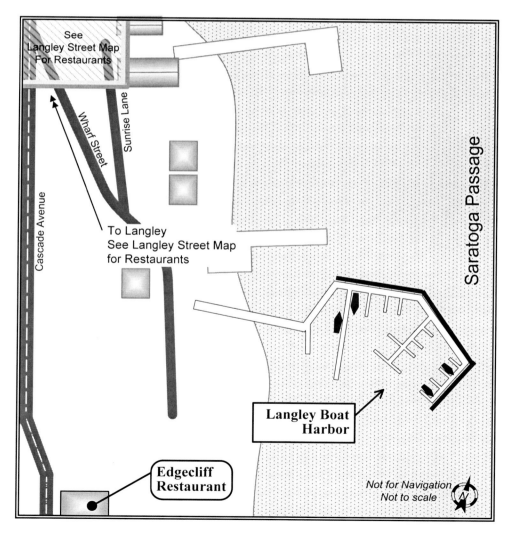

See Langley Street Map For Restaurants

Wharf Street

Sunrise Lane

Cascade Avenue

To Langley
See Langley Street Map
for Restaurants

Saratoga Passage

Langley Boat Harbor

Edgecliff Restaurant

Not for Navigation
Not to scale

LANGLEY
Langley Marina

LANGLEY RESTAURANTS			🍽
Braeburn	Breakfast, Salads, Sandwiches, Desserts	197 Second St.	360-221-3211
Café Langley	Seafood, Meats, Sandwiches, Pasta	113 First Street	360-221-3090
Chef's Dining Room	Seafood, Meat Dishes (2-3 hr presentation)	400 First Street (Inn at Langley)	360-221-3033
Chef's Pantry	Deli Cheese, Salads, Sandwiches	112 ½ Anthens	360-221-2060 (lunch boxes)
Dog House Tavern	Burgers, Sandwiches	230 First Street	360-221-4595
Edgecliff Restaurant	Seafood, Lamb, Pasta Steak, Sandwiches	510 Cascade Ave	360-221-8899
Island Coffeehouse	Espresso, Pastries	124 Second St.	360-221-2414
Langley Bakery	Espresso, Pastries	221 Second St.	360-221-3525
Langley Liquor Store	State Liquor Store	221 Second #9A	360-221-4520
Mike's Place	Breakfast, Fish, Burgers, Ice Cream	219 First Street	360-221-6575
One Angle Place	Chocolates	138 Second St.	360-221-2728
Prima Bistro	Seafood, Veal, Lamb, Sandwiches	201 ½ First St.	360-221-4060
2nd Street Wine	Wine Shop	221 Second #2A	360-221-3121
Star Store Market	Groceries	201 First Street	360-221-2468
Useless Bay Coffee	Espresso, Panini, Baked Goods	121 Second St.	360-221-4515
Village Pizzeria	Pasta, Pizza, Sandwiches	108 First Street	360-221-3363

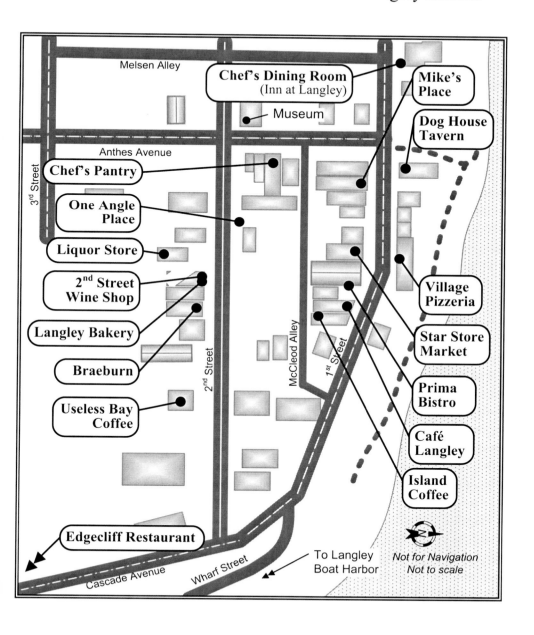

Melsen Alley

Chef's Dining Room
(Inn at Langley)

Mike's Place

Museum

Dog House Tavern

Anthes Avenue

3rd Street

Chef's Pantry

One Angle Place

Liquor Store

2nd Street Wine Shop

Langley Bakery

Braeburn

Useless Bay Coffee

2nd Street

McCleod Alley

1st Street

Village Pizzeria

Star Store Market

Prima Bistro

Café Langley

Island Coffee

Edgecliff Restaurant

Cascade Avenue

Wharf Street

To Langley Boat Harbor

Not for Navigation
Not to scale

LANGLEY
Langley Marina

EDGECLIFF RESTAURANT

The Edgecliff Restaurant is perched on the cliff above the Langley Boat Harbor with stunning views of Saratoga Passage and the Cascade Mountains. Once you reach the top of the road from the Boat Harbor, turn left and walk to the white-washed house at 510 Cascade Avenue. The lovely restaurant sports a peach, cream, and green color scheme with black tablecloths and white linen napkins, a romantic setting complete with an outstanding view. The menu is first class as well, including the Sea Salt Crusted Rack of Lamb served with potato au gratin, asparagus,

Lunch	11:30am – 4pm Daily
Dinner	4pm – 8:30pm Sun-Thur 4pm – 9:30pm Fri & Sat Hours Vary Off Season
Price	Moderate - Expensive
Outdoor Seating	Yes, Lawn Area, Summer Months
Contact	360-221-8899

and a port mint sauce; or try the Pan Seared Stuffed Chicken Breast, or perhaps the Seafood Stew with prawns, scallops, mussels, and Dungeness crab in a curried coconut orange broth. Lunch is equally pleasing with fresh salads and sandwiches, like the Cajun Chicken Sandwich, the Lamb Gyro, and Fish Taco. The Edgecliff is a romantic, relaxing venue any time of day.

PRIMA BISTRO

The Prima Bistro is located in the heart of Langley above the Star Store accessed by a narrow flight of stairs and overlooks First Street and Saratoga Passage from the rooftop patio. This intimate bistro with red furnishings and modern art work is the perfect venue for lunch or dinner. Start with a house-made pate' or a cheese plate, or perhaps mixed greens with Oregon blue cheese or cypress grove chevre to ready your palette for the luncheon Quiche du jour. Summer Squash & Mascarpone Risotto are other good choices for lunch.

Lunch	11:30am – 3pm Daily
Dinner	5pm – 9:30pm Sun-Thur 5pm – 10pm Fri & Sat Hours Vary Off Season
Price	Moderate
Outdoor Seating	Yes, Rooftop Patio, Summer Months
Contact	360-221-4060

The dinner menu changes every four to six weeks and may include the Roasted Free Range Chicken Breast with polenta, braised endive, rosemary, and gorgonzola pan jus; or try the Boudin Blanc, a house-made veal and pork sausage with Walla Walla onions served with a salad of new potatoes, celery, and whole grain mustard vinaigrette. The Prima Bistro offers special wine tasting events throughout the year and presents live entertainment by local musicians during the winter months. This Bistro expresses all the charm of Langley, not to be missed.

CAFÉ LANGLEY

Café Langley has all the charm of this seaside village offering cozy tables, antique furnishings, and lace curtains. Quality dishes served at Café Langley include the Penn Cove Mussels, the Mediterranean Seafood Stew, and the Dungeness Crab Cakes; or choose one of the Vegetarian or meat dishes like the Vegetarian Sampler or the tender Grilled Lamb. Another excellent choice is the Grilled Flank Steak served with pancetta, ale, roasted pepper sauce, and a side of roasted corn and pepper relish.

Lunch	11:30am – 2:30pm Mon-Thur 11:30am – 3pm Fri-Sun
Dinner	5pm – 8pm Sun-Thur 5pm – 9pm Fri & Sat Hrs Vary Off Season
Price	Moderate
Outdoor Seating	No
Contact	360-221-3090

Sandwiches, fish, salads, and homemade "soup of the day" are offered at lunch. Café Langley is a great place to relax and "people watch" while enjoying any meal followed by a Russian Cream Raspberry dessert.

MUKILTEO
Mukilteo Public Dock

The public dock at Old Town Mukilteo consists of three 24-foot floats, which are located on the northeast side of the Mukilteo ferry landing tucked behind the ferry wall and pilings, next to Ivar's Restaurant. The floats are available to visiting boaters during the summer months beginning in May at no charge; the floats are removed in late September. Boaters should be aware that the docks at the boat launch at Lighthouse Park located on the southwest side of the ferry landing are for launch purposes only.

Ivar's Restaurant and two pubs are within steps of the seasonal guest floats. Additional restaurants are located a few blocks up the hill off the Mukilteo Speedway. Several shops are clustered around a lovely treed courtyard, including the Mukilteo Booksellers, Riley's Pizza & BrewHaus, and Whidbey's Coffee & Café. The nearby Tin Fish eatery has a nice patio with great views overlooking Puget Sound and don't miss the Rose Hill Chocolate Co., offering fine chocolates and ice cream. If you are visiting Mukilteo on a Wednesday, stop by the Farmers' Market held at Rose Hill Community Center (Lincoln Ave. & 3rd St.) from 3pm to 7pm, June through September. For groceries and souvenirs, visit Woody's Market near the Mukilteo Lighthouse.

Touring the Mukilteo Lighthouse is a must. This Victorian style lighthouse began operation in 1906. Built at the same time were the Keepers' houses along with a pump-house and windmill. The lighthouse was converted to electricity in 1927 and automated in 1979. Today, the light and foghorn are maintained by the Coast Guard as working aids to navigation. The buildings are open to the public from noon to 5pm on weekends and holidays, April through September, call 425-513-9602 for tour information.

The name "Mukilteo" is taken from a Native American name meaning "good camping ground," and is the site where the Point Elliott Treaty was signed by Governor Isaac Stevens in 1855 with representatives of 22 Native American tribes. In 1858, pioneers established settlement at Mukilteo and developed a trading post, lumber mill, cannery, and port of entry for trading ships.

Future plans for Mukilteo include development of a new ferry terminal to be located north of the present location. Plans include installing a fishing pier and a day moorage dock at the new ferry landing. Look for exciting new developments in Old Mukilteo's "good camping ground" over the next few years.

Mukilteo Public Dock	425-259-3164	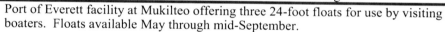
	Port of Everett Management	

Port of Everett facility at Mukilteo offering three 24-foot floats for use by visiting boaters. Floats available May through mid-September.

Short-Term: Hourly stays without charge while visiting Mukilteo and local restaurants.

Overnight: No overnight stays.

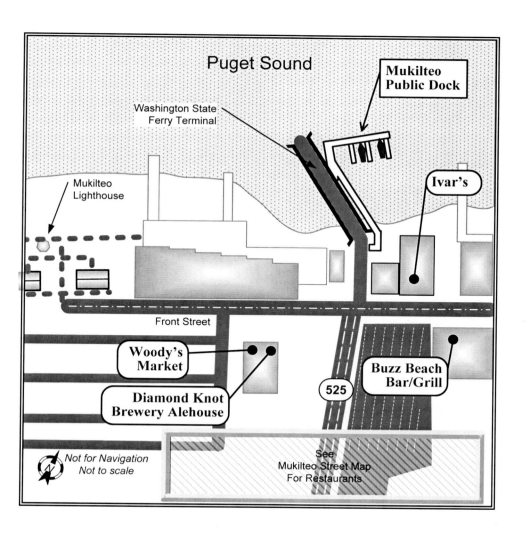

MUKILTEO
Mukilteo Public Dock

MUKILTEO RESTAURANTS			🍽
Arnies	Seafood, Meat, Pasta	714 Second St.	425-355-2181
Diamond Knot Brewery Alehouse	Sandwiches, Pizza, Soups, Appetizers	621A Front St.	425-355-4488
Diamond Knot Lincoln	Chicken, Pasta, Pizza, Salads	625 Fourth St.	425-512-8080
Ivar's Restaurant	Seafood, Sandwiches	710 Front Street	425-742-6180
John's Grill	Seafood, Meats	649 5th St. #101	425-347-1068
La Cascada Acapulco	Mexican Cuisine	801 Second St.	425-348-9569
Leely's Day Spa & Wine Shop	Wine Sales (spa services)	700 Third St. #E	425-268-6004
Rose Hill Chocolate	Ice Cream, Chocolate	700 Third Street	425-353-1183
The Tin Fish	Tacos, Sandwiches, Fish 'n Chips	204 Lincoln Ave	425-353-9549
Whidbey's Coffee & Café	Sandwiches, Baked Goods, Espresso	619 Fourth St.	425-348-4825
Willows Edge Tea Room	Sandwiches, Pasta, Entrees, Desserts	415 Lincoln Ave	425-438-2092
Woody's Market (groceries, gifts)	Breakfast Items, Hot Dogs, Soup, Pizza, Ice Cream	621B Front St.	425-347-6004

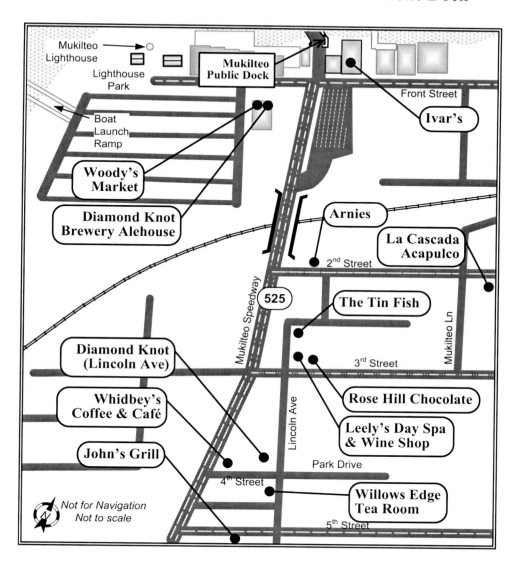

MUKILTEO
Mukilteo Public Dock

ARNIES 🍽

Arnies, located at the corner of Second Street and the Mukilteo Speedway, has commanding views of Puget Sound and the Mukilteo Lighthouse. You can enjoy all the boating activity from the large outdoor deck or from the dining room's picture windows. Arnies specializes in fresh fish, meat, and produce of the Northwest, including steak, pork, chicken, and seafood dishes. Try the Northwest Seafood Fettuccine, the Slow Roasted Prime Rib, or the house Smoked Pit Roasted Salmon with lemon beurre blanc and fried capers.		
	Lunch	11am – 4pm Mon-Fri
	Dinner	4pm – 9pm Sun-Thur 4pm – 9:30pm Fri & Sat
	Brunch	10am – 2pm Sundays
	Price	Moderate - Expensive
	Outdoor Seating	Yes, Deck, Summer Months
	Contact	425-355-2181

Arnies is the perfect venue for Sunday Brunch as well, which includes a selection of seasonal fruit, house-made sticky buns, and orange juice or Champagne with choice of entrée from the breakfast or lunch menu. Breakfast choices include French toast, waffles, omelettes, and Eggs Benedict. Visitors and locals alike love Arnies casual fare, linen-set tables, and beautiful views.

IVAR'S RESTAURANT 🍽

Ivar's, located on the waterfront next to the Mukilteo ferry landing, offers a beautiful dining room with close up views of the ferry traffic and the Mukilteo guest dock from window-side seating and from the summer deck. The restaurant is nicely appointed with warm woods, wainscoting, and a cozy fireplace. The separate Boathouse Lounge offers a more casual area for informal gatherings or you can order fish 'n chips at the street-side take-out window. Start your meal with Ivar's famous Clam Chowder or the Dungeness Crab Bisque with a hint of sherry, or perhaps the		
	Lunch/ Dinner	11am – 9pm Sun-Thur 11am – 10pm Fri & Sat
	Lounge	11am – 11pm Daily
	Price	Moderate - Expensive
	Outdoor Seating	Yes, Deck, Summer Months
	Contact	425-742-6180

Combination Seafood Salad with blackened wild salmon, baby prawns, and bay scallops in a house green goddess dressing. Ivar's classics include the Wild Northwest Salmon, the Halibut Fish 'n Chips, King Crab Legs, and the Mukilteo Seafood Stew. Sandwiches are always a nice option for lunch like the Wild Cod Fish Taco, the Crab Melt, or the Albacore Tuna Spring Roll. Ivar's restaurants, founded by Ivar Haglund in 1938, continue to be a Northwest favorite.

WILLOWS EDGE TEA ROOM

The Willows Edge Tea Room offers High Tea and Light Luncheons. The Tea Room is located in a charming white cottage with green trim and a hedged garden at 415 Lincoln Avenue. Tea is served with fresh scones and crème fraiche in the parlor decorated with pretty home furnishings and china. The "Petite Tea" includes sweets, a scone, fresh fruits, and a few bites of Country English Cheddar, while the "High Tea" includes sandwiches, a savory puff pastry, fresh fruits, and sweets.

Hours	11am – 4pm Wed-Sat 12:30pm – 3:30pm Sun Special Hrs. by Appt.
Price	Moderate - Expensive
Outdoor	Yes, Lawn, Summer Months
Contact	425-438-2092

The lunch menu offers soups, salads, Cornish beef pasties, and sandwiches like the Roast Chicken with fresh grapes, toasted walnuts, and cranberries & greens; or try the Roasted Butternut Squash Soup, a house favorite. Don't miss the French Chocolate Cake for dessert, a classic bittersweet chocolate delight served with a marionberry-raspberry coulis and a dollop of crème fraiche.

PORT HADLOCK
Irondale Dock

The Irondale Public Dock is located northwest of the Port Hadlock Marina at the south end of Port Townsend Bay. Boaters often miss this dock on the northwest bank of Port Hadlock, which provides hourly moorage for patrons of one of the most unique dining venues in all of Puget Sound. The Irondale Public Dock is a Port Townsend facility with approximately 75 feet of guest space for short-term stays at no charge on a first come, first serve basis. Boaters should note that the Irondale Dock may be busy during the Hadlock Days Celebration (360-379-5380) in mid-July.

The unique Ajax Café is within steps of the Public Dock and is housed in the historic Galster House built in the late 1800's. This house was once the home of Samuel Hadlock, the founder of Port Hadlock. Samuel came to Port Townsend Bay in 1870 after building the Tacoma lumber mill and serving as superintendent. Samuel built a new sawmill on the Port Hadlock waterfront around which was a general store, post office, hotels, and saloons. The sawmill ceased operation in 1907 and burned to the ground in 1913. The Galster's lived in the Hadlock home until 1949 where Mr. Glaster tended bar in the saloon located on the first floor of the house, which is now the Ajax Café.

Today, the Irondale waterfront is home to the well respected Northwest School of Wooden Boatbuilding (360-385-4948). Thousands of students have graduated from the School's vocational programs and summer workshops and come from around the world. The School has 14,500 square feet of covered space, including the historic two-story Captain Westrem Building and the fully restored Community Boathouse. Guided tours are available Monday through Friday at 10am and at 3pm, inquire at the administration office in the Westrem Building.

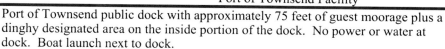

Irondale Public Dock	360-385-2355	
	Port of Townsend Facility	

Port of Townsend public dock with approximately 75 feet of guest moorage plus a dinghy designated area on the inside portion of the dock. No power or water at dock. Boat launch next to dock.

Short-Term: Hourly stays without charge; first come, first serve with a maximum stay of (2) 12-hour visits per month.

Overnight: No overnight stays. Anchorage nearby.

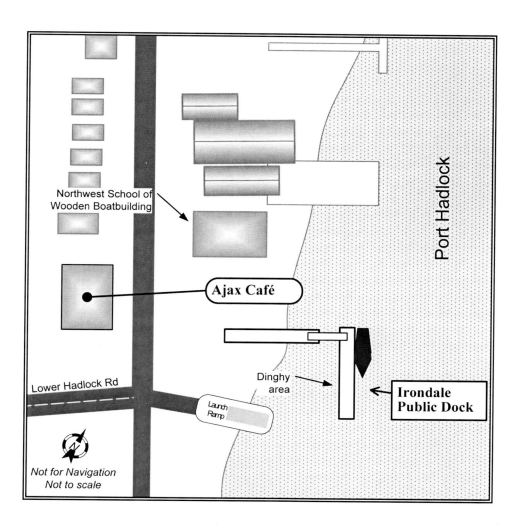

PORT HADLOCK
Irondale Dock

AJAX CAFE

Ajax Café is got to be one of the most unique and fun restaurants in all of Puget Sound. The historic 1800's house is just the beginning. We affectionately call Ajax "the hat place." Every night is hat night and folks can bring their own hat of choice, or simply choose one of the many hats from the walls around the Café ranging from period hats and career hats to national hats and comical hats. It is one happy party at Ajax with lively conversation spreading from table to table examining everyone's hat of choice.

Dinner	5pm – 9pm Daily June - August 5pm – 8pm Tue-Sun Off Season
Price	Moderate
Outdoor Seating	Yes, Patio, Summer Months
Contact	360-385-3450

Live entertainment at the piano with accompanying instruments completes the mood of an earlier time. The menu offers quality dishes which change seasonally along with nightly specials to include local fresh seafood, meats, fruits, and vegetables. Try the Grilled Chicken Risotto with sautéed wild mushrooms, zucchinis, and spinach topped with Asiago; or the Smoked Duck Salad served with roasted beets, pecans, and Boursin cheese and mixed baby greens tossed with shallot sherry vinaigrette. Old record albums are used for menu jacket covers; while reading the album cover, don't miss dessert like the Marionberry Pie. Reservations are a must at the infamous Ajax Café.

*Dress warmly for
the ride home*

PORT HADLOCK
Port Hadlock Marina

Port Hadlock is located at the south end of Port Townsend Bay just northwest of the Port Townsend/Hadlock Canal. The Port Hadlock Resort and Marina offers transient moorage and fine dining at Nemo's Restaurant housed in "The Inn at Port Hadlock," which once served as an alcohol plant. The Inn offers nice accommodations (360-385-7030) and therapeutic treatments at "The Spa" (360-379-1312) or you can visit The Art Mine Gallery (360-379-8555) located in the Inn next to the foyer. Transient moorage at Port Hadlock Marina is provided in unoccupied slips as available during the summer months at $1 per foot per day. Boaters should call ahead for availability and slip assignment prior to arrival or check the list of available slips posted at the head of the docks next to the self-registration payment box and Harbor Master Office.

The buildings serving as the Port Hadlock Resort were constructed in 1909 with thick steel I-beams and rebar for the Classen Chemical Co. (1910-1913), which produced ethyl alcohol from sawdust using a French distilling process, the Berigus Process. The distillation yielded fused oil, industrial ethyl alcohol, and spent wort used for cattle feed. The Alcohol Plant was established by Charles Adams, father of the famous photographer, Ansel Adams. Be sure to check out the photos of this historic site displayed in the hallway near the restaurant.

Port Hadlock Marina	360-385-6368 VHF 16/68
	360-531-0411 Harbor Master

Port Hadlock Marina offers guest moorage in unoccupied slips when available during the summer months, call ahead for availability. Restrooms, showers, laundry, pump-out. Power and water at dock.

Short-Term: 2 hour stay without charge, call ahead for available space.

Overnight: Overnight stays at $1 per foot per night, call ahead for availability, use self-registration payment box at head of dock. Anchorage nearby.

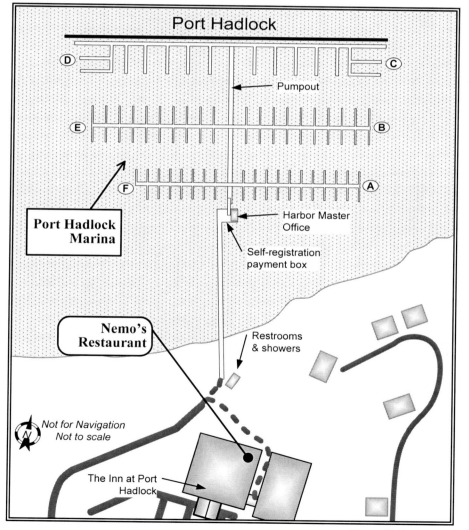

PORT HADLOCK
Port Hadlock Marina

NEMO'S RESTAURANT

Nemo's Restaurant has commanding views of Port Hadlock overlooking the Marina from the lovely garden patio and from the dining room's large picture windows. Be sure to note the metal and glass art pieces throughout the Inn and on the lovely grounds. Nemo's is the perfect stop for lunch offering sandwiches, burgers, fish, and pasta dishes. Dinner entrees incorporate local beef, chicken, and seafood like the coriander Dusted Seared Salmon, served with a leek risotto, arugala salad, and a roasted red bell pepper coulis.

Lunch	11am – 4pm Daily
Dinner	4pm – 8pm Sun-Thur 4pm – 9pm Fri & Sat Hrs Vary Off Season
Price	Moderate
Outdoor Seating	Yes, Patio, Summer Months
Contact	360-379-3333

The Grilled Black Angus Sirloin in an herb whiskey demi glace served with roasted potatoes and arugala salad is also a good choice. Visitors can stop by the Martini Bar for drinks and appetizers or enjoy one of Nemo's dessert selections like the Crème Brulee or the Key Lime Cheesecake.

PORT HADLOCK
Port Hadlock Marina

PORT LUDLOW
Port Ludlow

Port Ludlow has that peaceful, quiet appeal with outstanding views and excellent restaurants within steps of the Marina. Port Ludlow is located northwest of Port Gamble on Admiralty Inlet and is home to folks who enjoy this well planned seaside community of homes and condominiums with amenities including the Marina, the "Inn at Port Ludlow" (360-437-7000) and the Port Ludlow Golf Course. The Marina offers 50 guest slips and 350 feet of side-tie at a $1 per foot, reservations are highly recommended. Stays up to 4 hours are without charge if golfing or dining at the Resort and is on a first come, first serve basis. If arriving after hours, use the self-registration payment boxes located at the fuel dock and at the Marina Office; the Office stays open till 7pm Sunday-Thursday and until 9pm on Fridays and Saturdays, May through September and closes at 5pm during the off season.

The Resort offers the classy Fireside Restaurant located in the prestigious five-star Inn. Groceries and gifts can be purchased at the Marina Store/Office. Additional restaurants are located nearby at the Village Center, a pleasant three-quarter mile walk from the Marina. Trail maps of the area, including scenic Ludlow Falls, can be obtained from the Marina Office. If you wish to play the 27-hole, Port Ludlow Golf Course (360-437-0272), you can arrange for free shuttle service through the Marina Office. After a game of golf, you can enjoy some eats at Niblick's Café, conveniently located at the Pro Shop.

The planned community and resort at Port Ludlow was formalized in the 1960's by the Pope & Talbot Company, which had maintained a sawmill here until the mid 1900's. When the sawmill was dismantled, most of the old homes were loaded onto barges and transported to Port Gamble and Silverdale. The Inn, townhomes, and condominiums now stand where the sawmill once stood. The round foundation for one of the smokestacks is now a planter and the Totem Pole is where one of the refuse burners once stood. Pope & Talbot purchased the Port Ludlow Mill in 1878 from William Sayward and John Thorndyke, who had previously built the mill in 1852. This tiny community was also known for shipbuilding; and in the late 1800's, Hall Brothers Shipyards of Port Ludlow had completed 31 sailing ships.

Future plans for the Resort include demolishing the Harbormaster restaurant building (currently closed) in order to develop new condos on the property. The current Marina Office site will be redeveloped as well to house a new office, store, and restaurant with two condos on the upper level scheduled to start in 2010.

Port Ludlow Marina	360-437-0513 VHF 68
	www.portludlowresort.com

Port Ludlow marina with 50 guest slips and 350 feet of side-tie for hourly and overnight stays. Restrooms, showers, laundry, pumpout. Power and water on docks. Pavilion tent for groups. Fuel Dock.

Short-Term: 4 hours stay without charge if using the golf course or dining at the Resort; first come, first serve.

Overnight: Overnight stays at approx. $1 per foot depending on length of vessel; reservations recommended. Anchorage nearby.

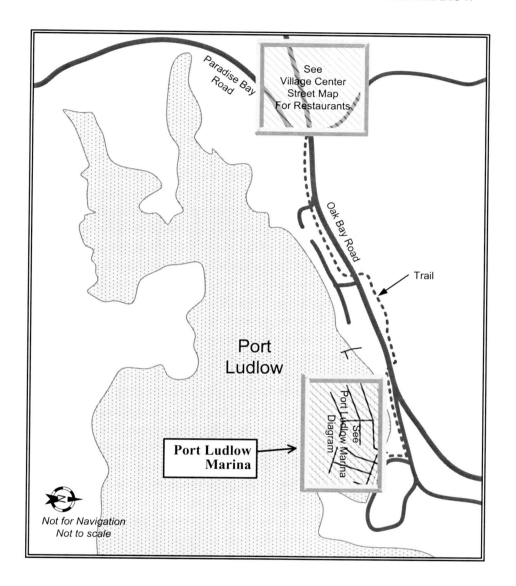

Paradise Bay Road

See
Village Center
Street Map
For Restaurants

Oak Bay Road

Trail

Port
Ludlow

See
Port Ludlow Marina
Diagram

**Port Ludlow
Marina**

Not for Navigation
Not to scale

PORT LUDLOW
Port Ludlow

PORT LUDLOW RESTAURANTS			🍽
Cucina Pizza	Pizza, Salads, Burgers, Pasta	52 Village Way	360-437-8200 (deliveries)
Niblick's Café	Burgers, Fish, Sandwiches	751 Highland Dr Golf Club	360-437-8276
Port Ludlow Marina Store	Groceries, Gifts	Marina Office	360-437-0513 877-344-6725
Port Ludlow Coffee	Espresso, Gifts, Pastries	44 Village Way	360-437-1133
Port Ludlow Market	Groceries, Deli	40 Village Way	360-437-9110
Snug Harbor Café	Breakfast, Seafood, Sandwiches, Tacos	9526 Oak Bay Road	360-437-8072
The Fireside	Breakfast, Seafood, Steak, Lamb	Inn at Port Ludlow Ludlow Resort	360-437-7000 877-805-0868

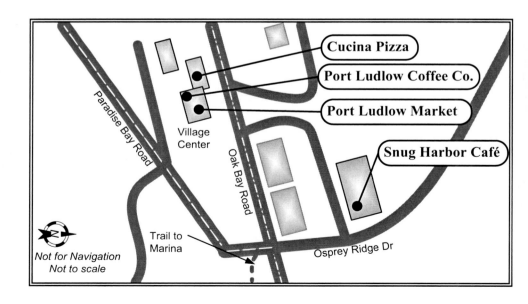

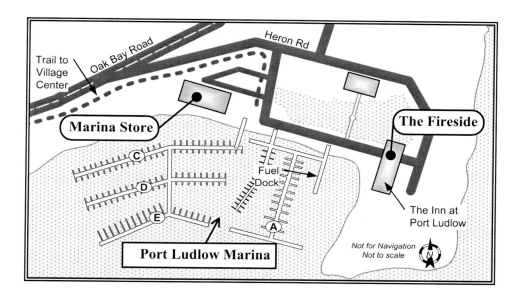

Trail to
Village
Center

Oak Bay Road

Heron Rd

Marina Store

The Fireside

C

D

E

Fuel
Dock

A

The Inn at
Port Ludlow

Port Ludlow Marina

Not for Navigation
Not to scale

N

PORT LUDLOW
Port Ludlow

THE FIRESIDE

The Fireside restaurant is located in the beautiful Inn at Port Ludlow, offering fine dining in a relaxing parlor around a double-sided fireplace. Beautiful sunsets over the Olympic Mountains add to the cozy, romantic setting; and the lovely white-washed veranda overlooking the Marina serves as an ideal summer venue. The menu offers Northwest cuisine using readily available fresh meats and seafood like the Wild King Salmon with Chardonnay reduction served with wild mushroom and leek risotto.

Breakfast	7am – 11pm Daily
Lunch	11am – 4pm Daily
Dinner	4pm – 9pm Daily Hrs Vary Off Season
Price	Moderate - Expensive
Outdoor Seating	Yes, Veranda, Summer Months
Contact	360-437-7000

Other delectable dishes include the pan seared Halibut, the Roasted Rack of Lamb, and the Oregon Natural Beef Tenderloin to name just a few of the fine choices. Special 4-course and 3-course dinners are offered on various nights like the French Bistro dinner on Tuesdays; Steak Night on Wednesdays; and the Italian Family Style dinners on Thursdays. Lunch selections include sandwiches, pasta dishes, and salads like the Spicy Beef Salad and the Capellini Scampi. Breakfast at the Inn is another option providing an early morning charm at Port Ludlow and includes traditional and specialty breakfast items.

PORT TOWNSEND
Port Townsend

Port Townsend is without question a destination with much to offer including parks, museums, marinas, public wharves, historic buildings, and numerous casual eateries and fine dining venues in addition to unique shopping and seasonal events. Boaters have several options for transient moorage: The Point Hudson Marina, the Union Wharf, the City Dock, and the Port Townsend Boat Haven. Point Hudson Marina is located on the northeast end of downtown and is within walking distance of shops and restaurants and offers 32 transient slips and 600 feet of side-tie with rafting permitted. Reservations are accepted with a $7 fee with rates based on vessel length or slip size, whichever is greater. The Marina Office is generally open from 8am to 5pm daily and is located in the small white building to starboard. The Union Wharf and the City Dock are both centrally located along the waterfront and within steps of the heart of Port Townsend. Both public docks have a maximum stay of 24 hours, no fees or reservations taken. Be sure to use spring lines as these docks are exposed to wind and waves. Port Townsend Boat Haven is located southwest of the central waterfront with a Safeway nearby. Guest space is in unoccupied slips along with 900 feet of side-tie on a first come, first serve basis. When entering the Boat Haven continue past the Coast Guard Station and tie-up at the fuel/registration dock and check in at the moorage office at the head of the ramp. Fees are based on vessel length or slip size, whichever is greater. Office hours are 8am to 4:30pm weekdays, and until 6:30pm on weekends; available slips are posted at the office door after hours. Temporary stays up to 4 hours with a $5 landing fee may be available at the fuel/registration dock. The Boat Haven is conveniently located on the Jefferson Co. Transit (360-385-4777) bus route to downtown Port Townsend.

In addition to enjoying the many fine restaurants in Port Townsend, you won't want to miss visiting Fort Worden State Park, a historic World War I military fort. Several points of interest are located within the Park: the Coast Artillery Museum in Building 201 (360-385-0373), the Marine Science Center on the Park's pier (360-385-5582), and self-guided tours of the Commanding Officer's Quarters (360-344-4400). During the summer months, music lovers flock to Fort Worden for annual music festivals and workshops. A guest dock (360-385-4730) with 128 feet of space for boats up to 25 feet in length plus 8 mooring buoys are available to boaters for hourly and overnight stays at 50 cents per foot, while visiting the Park located on the northern side of Port Townsend. Registration and payment box at head of dock.

Settlers first came to Port Townsend in 1851 and by the late 1800's the town was a well-known seaport. Many of the buildings were built on the speculation that the town would become a booming shipping port and major city. When the Depression hit and the rail lines ended on the east side of Puget Sound, many people left the area. Most of the abandoned structures were uninhabited until the 1970's; these buildings were kept in-tact and restored. Port Townsend is one of only three Victorian seaports on the National Register of Historic Sites. Most of Port Townsend's cafes and coffee shops are housed in these historic buildings accessed through side-doors, hallways, underground levels, and stairways leading to second floors. The rustic nature of these cafés is all part of the historic charm of Port Townsend.

Additional shops, restaurants, and the seasonal Farmers' Market can be found in Uptown, which is accessed via a set of stairs off Taylor Street. Two fine dining venues worth visiting in Uptown are Sweet Laurette Café (360-385-4886), and the Castle Key (360-385-5750) accessible via taxi. Numerous Victorian homes are located in this area overlooking the sea from the bluff above. You can pick up a town map from the Jefferson Co. Historical Museum (360-385-1003) in downtown at 540 Water Street.

Port Townsend attracts many visitors and hosts numerous festivals, concerts, regattas, and other events throughout the year. Opening Day Celebrations (360-385-3628) for boating season, which is held in early May, and the popular Wooden Boat Festival (360-385-3628) held in early September draw boating enthusiasts from far and wide. More than 150 classic wooden boats are featured in the Annual Wooden Boat Festival along with workshops, lectures, exhibits, shop tours, and family activities held at Point Hudson Harbor.

Be sure to allow plenty of time to take in all that Port Townsend has to offer. To access points of interest and sites beyond walking distance, call the Peninsula Taxi (360-385-1872) or use the Jefferson Co. Transit bus service (360-385-4777).

Point Hudson Marina

360-385-2828   VHF 66A

www.portofpt.com

Hudson Point marina with 32 transient slips and 600 feet of side-tie for guest moorage. Restrooms, showers, laundry. Power and water at docks. Launch ramp. Customs clearance (360-385-3777) with prior arrangement.

Short-Term: $5 fee for up to 4-hours, call ahead for availability and space.

Overnight: Reservations accepted with a $7 fee, rates are $1 per foot May-September and .80 per foot off season. Anchorage nearby.

City Dock

360-344-3055 Parks Dept.

City of Port Townsend 100 foot dock offering guest moorage and a 30 minute loading zone. Rafting at own risk. No power or water at dock. Dock/float removed in off season, available May-Sept.

Short-Term: Hourly stays without charge; first come, first serve.

Overnight: Overnight stay without charge with a 24-hour maximum stay in a 7-day period; first come, first serve. Anchorage nearby.

Union Wharf

360-344-3055 Parks Dept.

City of Port Townsend wharf with 130 foot dock for guest moorage and a striped area for dinghies and kayaks. No power or water at dock. Dock/float removed in off season, available May-Sept.

Short-Term: Hourly stays without charge; first come, first serve.

Overnight: Overnight stay without charge with a 24-hour maximum stay and an 80 foot maximum boat length. Anchorage nearby.

Port Townsend Boat Haven

360-385-2355   VHF 66A

360-385-7031 Fuel

Port of Port Townsend facility with transient space in unoccupied slips and 900 feet of side-tie; first come, first serve. Restrooms, showers, laundry, pumpout. Power and water at docks, Fuel dock. Customs clearance with prior arrangement.

Short-Term: $5 fee for short term up to 4 hours if available, while shopping at Safeway.

Overnight: First come, first serve; rates are .75 per foot. Anchorage nearby.

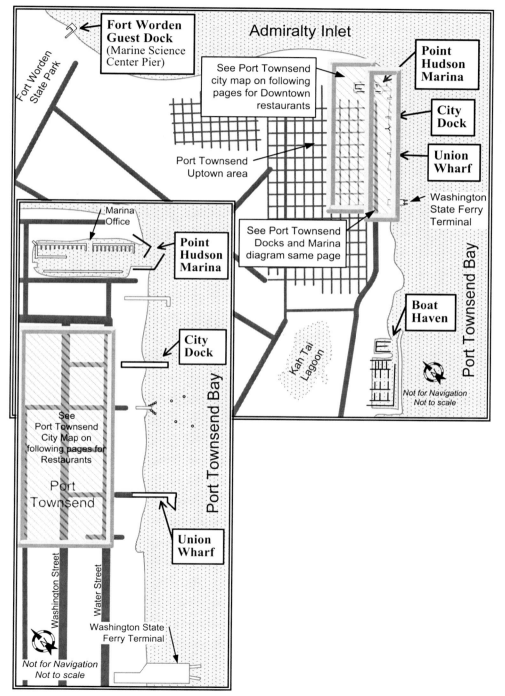

Fort Worden
Guest Dock
(Marine Science
Center Pier)

Admiralty Inlet

Point
Hudson
Marina

City
Dock

Union
Wharf

Fort Worden
State Park

See Port Townsend
city map on following
pages for Downtown
restaurants

Port Townsend
Uptown area

Washington
State Ferry
Terminal

See Port Townsend
Docks and Marina
diagram same page

Marina
Office

Point
Hudson
Marina

City
Dock

Port Townsend Bay

Boat
Haven

Kah Tai
Lagoon

Port Townsend Bay

Not for Navigation
Not to scale

See
Port Townsend
City Map on
following pages for
Restaurants

Port
Townsend

Union
Wharf

Washington Street

Water Street

Washington State
Ferry Terminal

Not for Navigation
Not to scale

PORT TOWNSEND RESTAURANTS 🍽			
Banana Leaf	Asian Bistro	609 Washington	360-379-6993
Belmont Restaurant & Saloon	Sandwiches, Pasta, Seafood, Meats	925 Water Street	360-385-3007
Courtyard Café	Baked Goods, Soups, Sandwiches, Coffee	230 Quincy	360-379-3355 (picnic boxes)
El Sarape	Mexican, Seafood	628 Water Street	360-379-9343
Elevated	Ice Cream, Candy	627 Water Street	360-385-1156
Fins Coastal Cuisine	Seafood, Pasta	1019 Water St.	360-379-3474
Fountain Café	Seafood, Sandwiches	920 Washington	360-385-1364
Galatea Café & Tapas Bar	Steak, Lamb, Brunch, Seafood, Tapas	842 Washington	360-385-5225
Hanazono	Asian Cuisine	225 Taylor Street	360-385-7622
Hudson Point Café (Otter Crossing Café)	Breakfast, Burgers, Sandwiches, Pasta	130 Hudson St.	360-379-0592
Jordini's Subs	Panini, Subs	929 Water St #D	360-385-2037 (deliveries)
Joy Luck	Chinese Cuisine	630 Water Street	360-379-1118
Khu Larb Thai	Thai Cuisine	225 Adams St.	360-385-5023
Lehani's	Organic Soups, Sandwiches, Coffee	221 Taylor St.	360-385-3961
Lighthouse Restaurant	Burgers, Fish, Salads, Sandwiches	955 Water Street	360-385-1165
Nifty Fifty's	Soda Fountain, Burgers	817 Water Street	360-385-1931
Public House Grill & Ales	Burgers, Steak, Seafood	1038 Water St.	360-385-9708

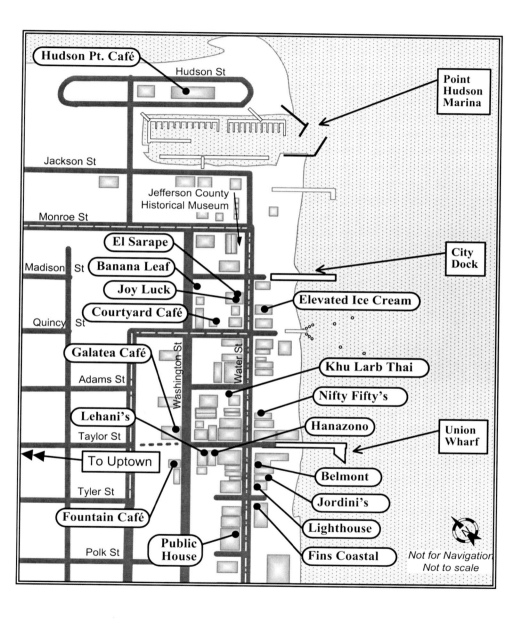

PORT TOWNSEND
Port Townsend

PORT TOWNSEND RESTAURANTS			🍽
Salal Café	Breakfast, Steak, Seafood, Burgers	634 Water Street	360-385-6532
Shanghai	Chinese Cuisine	Hudson Place	360-385-0660
Silverwater Café	Burgers, Panini, Chicken, Seafood	237 Taylor Street	360-385-6448
Sirens Pub (live music)	Burgers, Chicken, Seafood, Pizza	823 Water Street	360-379-1100
The Boiler Room	Coffee, Computer Work Space	711 Water Street	360-379-8247
The Landfall	Breakfast, Burgers, Sandwiches, Fish	412 Water Street	360-385-5814
The Spot Café	Soups, Meat Pies, Seafood, Salads	218 Polk	360-385-5275
Upstage (live music)	Seafood, Pasta, Steak	923 Washington	360-385-2216
Victorian Square Café & Deli	Breakfast, Wraps, Sandwiches, Salads	940 Water Street	360-385-6959
Water Street Brewing & Ale House	Brews, Pub Food	639 Water Street	360-379-6438
Waterfront Pizza	Pizza, Focaccia	953 Water Street	360-385-6629
Wine Seller	Wine Shop, Beer, and Tasting	1010 Water St.	360-385-7673

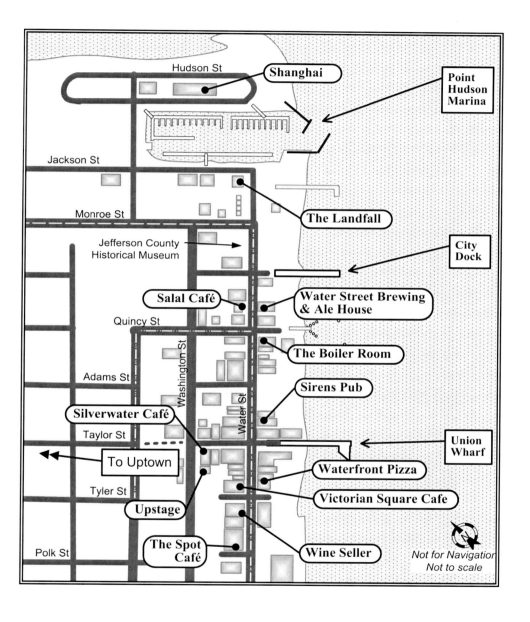

BELMONT RESTAURANT & SALOON 🍽️

The Belmont is Port Townsend's only remaining 1880's waterfront restaurant. Built in 1885 by George Sterming, the upper floor served as office suites and the ground floor housed the famous Belmont Saloon. Today, the office suites are Victorian style hotel rooms with 15-foot high ceilings with exposed brick walls, and the Belmont Restaurant continues to serve great food and drink as was reported in "The Port Townsend Leader" in the late 1800's. Patrons can enjoy beautiful views of the Bay from the large picture windows or from the outdoor deck during the summer months.

Lunch/	11:30am – 2:30pm Sun-Thur 11:30am – 4pm Fri & Sat
Dinner	4:30pm – 8pm Sun-Thur 4:30pm – 8:30pm Fri & Sat
Price	Moderate - Expensive
Outdoor Seating	Yes, Deck, Summer Months
Contact	360-385-3007

The extensive menu offers seafood and meat dishes, sandwiches, entrée salads, and pasta dishes. For lunch try the Crab & Artichoke Sandwich with onions and cheeses baked open-faced on Italian Panini bread, or try the Hot & Spicy Chicken Fettuccini. Dinner choices include Australian Lobster Tail, King Crab Legs, and Washington Halibut along with chicken, duck, lamb, and steak selections like the 16oz Black Angus Rib-eye prepared with Belmont's seasonal steak butter. Sit back, relax, and enjoy the ambiance of "yester-year" and share your adventures of today.

COURTYARD CAFÉ

The Courtyard Café is located on Quincy Street in a charming yellow house with green trim. This delightful café serves excellent espresso, soups, salads, and sandwiches. Classics include the Turkey Cranberry and the Egg Salad Sandwich, or try the Sauteed Veggie, or perhaps the Muffuletto with capicola ham, olive tapenade, and provolone cheese on a Panini. Don't forget to ask about the soup of the day or choose one of the tasty salads like the Pesto Chicken or the Warm Spinach Salad. Be sure to save room for the baked goods or one of the delectable crème pies.

Breakfast	7am – 11am Daily Sunday till Noon
Lunch	11am – 5pm Thur-Tue Closed Wednesdays Hrs Vary Off Season
Price	Moderate
Outdoor Seating	Yes, Porch Deck, Summer Months
Contact	360-379-3355

Breakfast is served daily, including waffles, quiche, and the Skillet Scramble, or you can enjoy a homemade crepe filled with sweetened crème cheese and fruit.

CASTLE KEY RESTAURANT

The Castle Key restaurant is located in the Manresa Castle at 7th & Sheridan southwest of downtown accessible via taxi. The Castle was completed in 1892 as the home of Charles and Kate Eisenbeis. Charles was a prominent businessman and the town's first mayor. The Castle was made with the brick's from Charle's brickworks and constructed with foot thick walls. In 1968 the building was converted into a hotel and renamed Manresa Castle.

Dinner	5pm – 9pm Tue-Sat
Brunch	9am – 1pm Sunday
Price	Moderate - Expensive
Outdoor Seating	No
Contact	360-385-5750

The restaurant occupies what was originally the parlor and dining rooms and has beautiful wood work, chandeliers, and coffered ceilings. Visitors and guests of the hotel are invited to enjoy Sunday brunch and dinners at this unique venue. For dinner, start with the Chef's seasonal soup creation or the Spinach Salad with fresh strawberries followed by the Filet Mignon, or try the Grilled Wild Salmon lightly covered in a raspberry Jalapeno sauce atop wilted spinach and Arborio rice. Brunch is a treat as well, including Pork Apple Cinnamon Sausage & Eggs, Praline French Toast, and other tasty selections.

FOUNTAIN CAFÉ

The Fountain Café is located off the beaten path on Washington Street near the Haller Fountain and stairway to Uptown. The Fountain Café has a friendly neighborhood feel sporting a colorful décor and a collection of local art. This cozy café is housed in the historic Mary Webster Building and has been featured in several travel guides. The creative menu includes fresh seafood, homemade pasta, gourmet sandwiches, and homemade desserts. Start with an appetizer like the Roasted Garlic with melted Brie and salsa fresco on toasted baguette or perhaps the Insalate Mista.

Lunch/ Dinner	11:30am – 3pm Daily 5pm – 9pm Sun-Thur 5pm – 9:30pm Fri & Sat Hours Vary Off Season
Price	Moderate
Outdoor Seating	No
Contact	360-385-1364

For the main course, try the Roasted Walnut and Gorgonzola Penne in a rich cream sauce with spinach and slow roasted tomatoes, or try the Wild Mushroom Risotto. Lunch favorites include the Tapenade Chicken Sandwich and the Classic Warm Salad with greens tossed in warm vinaigrette, potatoes, assorted veggies, and cappacollo, topped with parmesan, pine nuts, and French olives. You won't want to miss the homemade desserts like the Chocolate Tart with raspberry topping, or the Pear Tart, Crème Brulee, or the Gingerbread Cake.

Fuel Docks

Seattle Area Waters

Lake Washington
    Newport Fuel Dock, Bellevue   425-641-2090
    Northlake Marina, Kenmore   425-482-9465
    Yarrow Bay Marina, Kirkland   425-822-6066

Lake Union
    Morrison's North Star   206-284-6600

Ship Canal
    Ballard Oil   206-783-0241
    Covich-Williams   206-784-0171

Elliott Bay
    Elliott Bay Marina   206-282-8424
    Shilshole Marina Texaco   206-783-7555

Central Sound

Brownsville Marina   360-692-0687
Poulsbo Marina   360-779-3505
Port Orchard Marina   360-876-5535

North Sound

Edmonds Marina   425-774-0549
Everett Marina   425-259-6001
Kingston Marina   360-297-3545
Port Ludlow Marina   360-437-0513
Port Townsend (Boat Haven)   360-385-7031

Index

1

104 Trolley, 191
12 Street Yacht Basin, 181
122 Dining & Cheer, 127

2

21 Club, 13
2100 Bistro, 93, 94
24th Avenue Casual Dining, 83
24th Avenue Coffee & Desserts, 85
24th Avenue Fine Dining, 85
2nd Street Wine, 197

A

Acapulco Fresh Mexican Grill, 3
Agate Pass café, 151
AGC Building, 47
AGC Building Guest Dock, 48
Agua Verde Café, 43
Agua Verde Guest Dock, 42
Ajax Cafe, 209
Alki Crab & Fish, 99, 101
Alki Point Lighthouse, 99
Alki Pylon, 99
Amy's on the Bay, 169, 171
Andante Coffee, 125
Anne's Teriyaki, 83
Annual Fishing Kids, 37
Anthony's Beach Café, 175, 177
Anthony's Fish Bar, 93
Anthony's Homeport, 13, 105, 183, 184
Anthony's Pier 66, 93
Anthony's Pier 66 & Bell St. Diner, 94
Anthony's Restaurant, 161, 163, 175
Anthony's Woodfire Grill, 183
Apple Tree Deli, 191
Appletree Cove, 189
Argosy Cruises, 47
Arnies, 175, 178, 203, 205
Art Mine Gallery, 211

Aster Coffee, 85
Attic Alehouse & Eatery, 33
Aurora Valentinetti Puppet Museum, 159
Azteca, 69
Azteca Mexican, 83

B

Bainbridge, 121
Bainbridge Bakers, 125
Bainbridge City Restaurants, 125, 127
Bainbridge Historical Museum, 121
Bainbridge Island BBQ, 125, 131
Bainbridge Island Taxi, 121
Bainbridge Thai, 125
Bal Mar Lounge, 83
Ballard, 81
Ballard Seafood Fest, 81
Banana Leaf, 225
Bay Café, 77
BayShore Day Spa, 115
Bayside Broiler, 139
Beach Café, 21, 23
Beachfire Grill, 187
BeachHouse, 7
BeachHouse Guest Dock, 8
Bell Harbor Marina, 91, 92
Bell Harbor Marina Restaurants, 93
Bell Street Deli, 93
Bell Street Diner, 93
Bella Luna Pizzeria, 152
Belmont Restaurant, 225
Belmont Restaurant & Saloon, 229
Bin Vivant, 21, 23
Bing's, 33
Blackberry Festival, 159
Blackbird Bakery, 125
Blake Island, 109
Blake Island Marine Park, 110
BluWater Bistro, 21, 27, 29, 73, 75
Boat Shed, 157
Boat Shed Guest Dock, 156
Boatyard Inn, 195

Boehms Chocolates, 139
Bon Bon, 125
Boston's Pizza, 161
Boston's Pizza Deli, 165
Braeburn, 197
Bremerton, 159
Bremerton Restaurants, 161
Brownsville, 113
Brownsville Marina, 114
Brownsville Marine & Deli, 113
Bubbles, 99
Buca di Beppo, 67
Buca Di Beppo, 65
Bucksnort Coffee, 167
Burrata Bistro, 139

C

Cabin Museum, 167
Cactus, 11, 33, 35
Café Besalu, 85
Café Happy, 11
Café Harlequin, 13, 17
café Langley, 200
Café Langley, 197
Café Nola, 125
Café Pavilion, 125
Café Trios, 125
Caffe Appassionato, 77, 80
Caffe Ladro, 13
Calabria Ristorante, 13
Candy Shoppe, 169
Cargo Hold, 137
Carillon Point, 21
Carillon Point Guest Pier, 22
Carillon Point Restaurants, 21
Carlisle II Historic Ferry, 167
Carnegie's, 85
Casa Luna, 139
Casa Rojas, 125
Cascadia Nauticals, 195
Castle Key Restaurant, 231
Ce'fiore Yogurt, 13
Center for Wooden Boats, 55, 65
Chai House, 85
Chandler's Cove, 51
Chandler's Cove Guest Dock, 52

Index

Chandler's Cove Restaurants, 51
Chandler's Crabhouse, 51, 53
Checkers, 139
Chef's Dining Room, 197
Chef's Pantry, 197
Chief Seattle Days, 149
Chinooks, 77, 79
City Dock, 221, 223
Classic Cycle, 121
Coast Artillery Museum, 221
Coffee & Cone, 13
Coffee Exchange, 191
Cold Stone Creamery, 161
Cookin, 31
Corner Deli, 169
Coulon Park, 38
Courtyard Cafe, 230
Courtyard Café, 225
Coyote Creek Pizza, 11
Crab Cracker, 15
Cucina Pizza, 217
Cugini Café, 85

D

Daily Stop Grocery, 113
Daniel's Broiler, 27, 30, 51, 57
Daruma, 183
Delilah's, 169
Diamond Knot Brewery Alehouse, 203
Diamond Knot Lincoln, 203
Doc's Marina Grill, 125
Dog House Tavern, 197
Drifters Bar/Lounge, 191
Drifters Espresso Bar, 191
Duke's Chowder House, 51, 54
Dyes Inlet, 115

E

Eagle Harbor Marina, 123
Edgecliff Restaurant, 197, 199
Edmonds, 175
Edmonds Marina, 176
Edmonds Port Restaurants, 175
Edna's Beach Café, 121
El Sarape, 225
Electric Boat Water Taxi, 51, 59

Elevated, 225
Eleven Winery, 125
Elliott Bay Marina, 95, 96
Elliott Bay Water Taxi, 99
Emerald City Smoothie, 15
Emmy's VegeHouse, 125
Equator, 180
Everest Grocery & Deli, 3
Everett, 179
Everett Marine Park, 181
Everett Port Restaurants, 183

F

Faces of the NW, 175
Family Inn, 145
Filling Station Pub, 191
Fins Coastal Cuisine, 225
Fish Café, 13, 18
Fishermen's Fall Festival, 77
Fishermen's Grocery, 77
Fishermen's Memorial Foundation, 77
Fishermen's Terminal, 77, 78
Fishermen's Terminal Restaurants, 77
Flowering Around, 125
Fort Worden State Park, 221
Fountain Café, 225, 232
Four Swallows, 125, 129
Fraiche Cup, 161, 166
Freeland, 185
Fritz Fry House, 161

G

Galatea Café & Tapas Bar, 225
Gandhi, 125
George's Place, 11
Gino's, 169, 172
Golden Gardens Park, 103
Grape Expectations, 117
Great Harvest, 83

H

H.C. Henry Pier, 55, 56
Hadlock Days Celebration, 207
Hamburger Harry's, 83
Hanazono, 225
Hanuman Thai Café, 11

Harbor Public House, 125
Harbor Square Wine, 125
Harborside Fountain Park, 159
Harbour Marina, 123
Hector's, 11
Hellebore Glass Studio, 195
Hideaway Café, 169
Highliner Pub, 77
Hi-Life, 83, 87
Hoffman's, 15
Holmes Harbor, 185
Holmes Harbor Beach Club, 186
Hooters, 51
Hot Shots Java, 139
Hudson Point Café, 225
Husky Party Boat, 79

I

I Love Sushi, 73, 76
I Luv Teriyaki, 11
Impromptu, 33
Impromptu Café, 35
India Bistro, 85
Indianola Country Store & Deli, 147
Indianola Pier, 148
Inn at Langley, 195
Inn at Port Hadlock, 211
Inn at Port Ludlow, 215
Irondale, 207
Irondale Public Dock, 208
Isla Bonita, 127
Island Coffeehouse, 197
Ivar's Guest Dock, 60
Ivar's Restaurant, 203, 205
Ivar's Salmon House, 59, 61
Ivar's Seafood Bar, 39, 62

J

J.J.'s Fish House, 139, 141
J'aime Les Crepes, 191, 193
Jack in the Box, 3
Jalisco Mexican, 11
Java Bean, 85
Jefferson Co. Historical Museum, 222
Jefferson Co. Transit, 222
Jetty Island, 179

Index

Jetty Island Dock, 181
Jillian's, 65
Joeys, 51
John's Grill, 203
Jordini's Subs, 225
Joy Luck, 225
Juwapas, 169

K

Kahili Coffee, 13
Kenmore, 3
Kenmore Air, 4, 45
Kenmore Restaurants, 3
Keyport, 133
Keyport Mercantile, 135
Khu Larb Thai, 225
Kidd Valley, 39
Kids Discovery Museum, 121
Kingston, 189
Kingston Art Gallery, 189
Kingston Marina, 190
Kingston Restaurants, 191
Kirkland, 5
Kirkland Bicycle Shop, 9
Kirkland Casual Dining, 11
Kirkland Coffee & Dessert, 13
Kirkland Fine Dining, 13
Kirkland Heritage Society, 5
Kirkland Parkplace
    Restaurants, 15
Kitsap County Historical
    Society Museum, 159
Kitsap Transit, 121
Kitsap Transit Foot Ferry, 153

L

La Cascada Acapulco, 203
LaIsla, 83
Lai-Thai, 11
Lake Union, 45
Lake Washington, 3
Lakepointe Bar & Grill, 3
Langley, 195
Langley Bakery, 197
Langley Boat Harbor, 196
Langley Liquor Store, 197
Langley Restaurants, 197
Leely's Day Spa & Wine Shop,
    203

Lehani's, 225
Leschi, 27
Leschi Food Mart, 27
Leschi Landing, 28
Leschi Restaurants, 27
Liberty Bay, 133, 137
Liberty Bay Bakery, 139
Lighthouse Restaurant, 225
Little Chinooks, 77
Little Coney, 105
Log House Museum, 99
Lombardi's, 85, 183
Los Cabos, 169
Lucia, 15
Ludlow Falls, 215
Lumpia Teriyaki, 161
Luna Belle, 191
Lynn's Bistro, 13
Lynwood Center, 121

M

Mad Pizza, 33
Madame K's, 83
Madison Park, 31
Madison Park Bakery, 33
Madison Park Café, 33, 36
Madison Park Casual
    Restaurants, 33
Madison Park Coffee &
    Desserts, 33
Madison Park Fine Dining, 33
Madison Park Hardware, 31
Madison Park Landing, 32
Madoka, 127
Maggie Bluff's Marina Grill,
    97
Main Street Ale House, 191,
    194
Manchester, 143
Manchester Dock, 144
Manchester Food Center, 143
Manette, 155
Marina Market, 139
Marina Park Dock, 9
Marina Park Grill, 11
Marine Science Center, 221
Market Street Café, 13
Matador, 83, 88, 89
McCormick & Schmick's, 49
McGilvra's, 33
McGregor & Co., 115, 117

Meyer's Café, 183
Mike Wallace Park, 189
Mike's Place, 197
Miro Tea, 85
Mon Elisa's, 127
Monica's Bakery, 117
Monica's Waterfront Bakery,
    119
Mooberry, 85
Moon Dogs, 167, 169
Mor Mor Bistro, 139
Mor Mor Bistro & Bar, 142
Mora Iced Creamery, 127
Morningside Bakery, 169
Moshi Moshi, 83
Mukilteo, 201
Mukilteo Lighthouse, 201
Mukilteo Public Dock, 202
Mukilteo Restaurants, 203

N

Nattamit, 117
Naval Memorial Museum, 159
Naval Reserve Center, 45
Naval Undersea Museum, 133
Navy Warship Tours, 153, 159
Nemo's Restaurant, 213
New Delhi, 161
Niblick's Café, 217
Nifty Fifty's, 225
Noah's Bagels, 15
Nordic Heritage Museum, 81
Northlake Marina, 3
Northwest School of Wooden
    Boatbuilding, 207
Norwegian Constitution Day
    Parade, 81

O

O'Shun Sushi, 83
Oayaca, 83
Ocho, 83
Odyssey Maritime Discovery
    Center, 91
Officer's Quarters, 221
Old Town Ale, 83
Old Town Bistro, 117
Old Town Flowers, 117
Olympic Sculpture Park, 91

Index

One Angle Place, 197
Opening Day, 41
Opening Day Celebrations, 222
Other Coast Café, 83
Otter Crossing Café, 225
Outback Steak House, 65, 68

P

Pacific Parasail, 9
Palisade, 98
Papa Johns, 11
Park Place Deli, 33
Paseo, 105
Pegasus Coffee House, 127, 132
Peninsula Taxi, 222
People's Pub, 83
Pert's Deli, 27
Pho Than, 83
Pho Yummy, 25
Pike Place Market, 91
Pioneer Museum, 31
Point Hudson Marina, 221, 223
Poppinjay's Café, 21
Port Gardner Inn, 179
Port Hadlock, 211
Port Hadlock Marina, 212
Port Ludlow, 215
Port Ludlow Coffee, 217
Port Ludlow Golf Course, 215
Port Ludlow Marina, 215
Port Ludlow Marina Store, 217
Port Ludlow Market, 217
Port Ludlow Restaurants, 217
Port Madison, 147
Port of Bremerton Marina, 160
Port of Everett Marina, 181
Port of Keyport, 134
Port Orchard, 167
Port Orchard Bay, 153
Port Orchard Marina, 168
Port Orchard Pier, 167
Port Orchard Restaurants, 169
Port Townsend, 221
Port Townsend Boat Haven, 221, 223
Port Townsend Restaurants, 225, 227
Portage Bay, 41
Possession Sound, 179
Poulsbo, 137

Poulsbo Guest Marina, 138
Poulsbo Marine Science Center, 137
Poulsbo Restaurants, 139
Poulsbo Woodfired Pizza, 139
Poulsbohemian, 139
Prima Bistro, 197, 200
Public House Grill & Ales, 225
Puget Sound Maritime Historical Society, 51
Purple Café, 15, 20

R

Raga, 11
Ray's Boathouse, 105
Ray's Boathouse & Cafe, 106
Ray's Cafe, 105
Real Foods Café, 127
Red Apple Market, 33
Renton, 37
Rikki Rikki, 15
Ristorante Paradiso, 13, 19
Rock Salt Guest Dock, 64
Rock Salt Steak House, 63
Root Table, 83, 89
Rose Hill Chocolate, 203
Ruby Asian, 27

S

Saigon Jades, 15
Salal Café, 227
Salsa, 191
Salty's, 99, 102
Sam's Sushi, 83
San Carlos, 127
Santorini Greek Grill, 11
Saratoga Inn, 195
Saratoga Passage, 195
Scoop du Jour, 33
Scooter's, 83
Scuttlebutt Brewing, 183
Seacrest Park Dock, 100
Seacrest Park Restaurants, 99
Seattle, 91
Seattle Aquarium, 91
Second Avenue Dock, 10
Serafina, 69, 71
Settlers Landing, 26
Shanghai, 227

Sheila's Bay Café, 139
Shiku, 83
Shilshole Bay Marina, 103
Shilshole Bay Restaurants, 105
Shima Sushi, 127, 130
Shnoo Yogurt, 13
Siam Thai, 69, 72
Sidney Museum, 167
Silverdale, 115
Silverdale Guest Dock, 116
Silverdale Old Town Restaurants, 117
Silverwater Café, 227
Simon's, 127
Sinclair Inlet, 153
Sirens Pub, 227
Sluys Poulsbo Bakery, 139
Snoose Junction, 83
Snug Harbor Café, 217
Sogno di Vino, 139
Sostanza Trattoria, 33
South Lake Union Park, 65, 66
South Lake Union Park Restaurants, 65
South Lake Union Seawall, 65
South Pacific Sports Bar, 161
South Whidbey Historical Museum, 195
Spa Essencia, 195
Space Needle, 91
Spice Route, 127
St. James Espresso, 15
Star Store Market, 195, 197
Starbucks, 13, 15, 21, 27, 33, 49, 85, 93, 161
Streamliner Diner, 127
Subway, 127, 161
Sunny Teriyaki, 83
Suquamish, 149
Suquamish Guest Dock, 150
Suquamish Memorial Cemetery, 149
Sur La Table, 9
Sweeny's Country Style Meat Co., 113
Sweet Laurette Cafe, 222
SweetCakes, 13

T

Taco Del Mar, 11, 161
Taco Loco Baja, 161

Index

Teriyaki Town, 127
Terry Pettus Park, 70
Terry Pettus Park Restaurants, 69
TGI Fridays, 15
Thai Ginger, 33
Thaiku, 85
That's A Some Pizza, 127
That's-A-Some Italian, 139
The Boiler Room, 227
The Chandlery, 121
The Fireside, 217, 219
The French Bakery, 13
The Grape Choice, 13
The Landfall, 227
The Original Pancake House, 15
The Purple Cow, 105
The Red Onion, 33
The Slip, 11
The Spa, 211
The Spot Café, 227
The Tin Fish, 203
The Village Baker, 139
Tiki Joe's Wet Bar, 11
Tillicum Village Longhouse, 109, 111
Tim's Seafood, 15
Tin Cup Espresso, 65
Tizley's Europa, 139
Tokyo Grill, 11
Town & Country, 127
Tracy Owen Park Pier, 4
TreeHouse Café, 121
Trellis, 13

Trolley Café, 93
Tugboat Story Time, 65
Tully's, 33, 85

U

Underground Tour, 91
Union Wharf, 221, 223
Unlimited Light Hydroplane Races, 115
Upstage, 227

V

Vera's, 83
Verite Coffee, 85
Victorian Square Café & Deli, 227
Viking Fest, 137
Volterra, 85, 90
Voodiez Bar & Grill, 139
VoVina, 11

W

Water Street Brewing & Ale House, 227
Waterfront Café, 175
Waterfront Park Dock, 123
Waterfront Pizza, 227
Westside Pizza, 127, 191
Whaling Days, 115
Whidbey Island Moped, 195
Whidbey Island Winery, 195

Whidbey's Coffee & Café, 203
Whiskey Creek Ranch House, 139
Whiskey Creek Steakhouse, 136
Wilde Rover, 11
Wilde Rover Irish Pub, 20
Willows Edge Tea Room, 203, 206
Windermere Cup, 41
Wine Cellar, 169
Wine Seller, 227
Wing Dome, 11
Winslow, 121
Winslow Wharf Marina, 123
Wooden Boat Festival, 65, 222
Woodmark Hotel, 21
Woodmark Spa, 21
Woody's Market, 203

Y

Yacht Club Broiler, 117, 120
Yale Landing Restaurants, 73
Yale Street Landing, 73, 74
Yarrow Bay Grill, 21, 24
Yarrow Bay Marina, 21

Z

Zak's, 83
Zaw, 83
Zeek's Pizza, 11